JAMES JOYCE:
A PORTRAIT OF THE ARTIST AS A YOUNG MAN

by

HARVEY PETER SUCKSMITH
Associate Professor of English, Dalhousie University, Halifax, Nova Scotia

EDWARD ARNOLD

© Harvey Peter Sucksmith, 1973

First published 1973 by
Edward Arnold (Publishers) Ltd,
25 Hill Street, London W1X 8LL
Reprinted 1976
Cloth edition: ISBN 0 7131 5716 x
Paper edition: ISBN 0 7131 5717 8

00019777

Printed in Great Britain by
The Camelot Press Ltd, Southampton

LUTON SIXTH FORM COLLEGE

WITHDRAWN

−2. JUN. 1977	11. APR. 1978	
14. JUN. 1977	11. MAY 1978	
	29. JUN. 1978	
−8. SEP. 1977	12. DEC. 1983	
28. SEP. 1977	16. JUN. 1985	
20. OCT. 1977		
25. NOV. 1977	22. APR. 1986	
19. DEC. 1977	1 1 NOV 2016	
−9. JAN. 1978		
−3. FEB. 1978		
20. FEB. 1978		
16. MAR. 1978		

This book is due for return on or before the last date shown above.

3123

Already published in the series:

General Preface

The object of this series is to provide studies of individual novels, plays and groups of poems and essays which are known to be widely read by students. The emphasis is on clarification and evaluation; biographical and historical facts, while they may be discussed when they throw light on particular elements in a writer's work, are generally subordinated to critical discussion. What kind of work is this? What exactly goes on here? How good is this work, and why? These are the questions that each writer will try to answer.

It should be emphasized that these studies are written on the assumption that the reader has already read carefully the work discussed. The objective is not to enable students to deliver opinions about works they have not read, nor is it to provide ready-made ideas to be applied to works that have been read. In one sense all critical interpretation can be regarded as foisting opinions on readers, but to accept this is to deny the advantages of any sort of critical discussion directed at students or indeed at anybody else. The aim of these studies is to provide what Coleridge called in another context 'aids to reflection' about the works discussed. The interpretations are offered as suggestive rather than as definitive, in the hope of stimulating the reader into developing further his own insights. This is after all the function of all critical discourse among sensible people.

DAVID DAICHES

Contents

Acknowledgements

The author and publishers wish to thank the following for permission to quote in extract from copyright material: Jonathan Cape, Viking Press and the Executors of the James Joyce Estate (© 1964) for the Definitive Text of *A Portrait of the Artist as a Young Man*; Cape and New Directions Publishing Corporation for *Stephen Hero*, introduced by Theodore Spencer, revised by John J. Slocum and Herbert Cahoon (Norfolk, Connecticut, 1944, 1963 and London, 1956); Northwestern University Press for the 'Epiphany of Hell' from the manuscript at Cornell University and the manuscript essay, 'A Portrait of the Artist', at the University of Buffalo, both published in Richard M. Kain and Robert E. Scholes, *The Workshop of Daedalus* (Evanston, Illinois, 1965), and the Society of Authors, London, on behalf of the James Joyce Estate, for manuscript material; Oxford University Press for Richard Ellman, *James Joyce* (New York, 1959).

Introduction

A Portrait of the Artist as a Young Man may not be Joyce's greatest novel. It lacks, for example, the scale and scope of *Ulysses* or the mythopoeic and linguistic richness of *Finnegans Wake*. Yet it is Joyce's most exquisite work of fiction, perhaps his most perfect novel, and it is certainly the one which communicates with us most readily. Though Joyce always exercises a proper artistic economy, it might be said that, whereas in reading *Ulysses* we are persistently confronted by a luxury and extensiveness of experience, in reading *A Portrait of the Artist* we are constantly astonished by a marvellous compression of complex matter and meaning. Indeed, as we shall see, the compact complexity of this novel and its intricate organic structure are strikingly confirmed by the method it compels the critic to adopt; for he must often consider the same material (especially key passages) more than once to expose new levels of meaning and he must frequently disentangle and present only one level of meaning at a time to remain clear.

A Portrait of the Artist was first published in 1916. If we except *Stephen Hero*, an earlier version of *A Portrait* (some fragments of which were published only in 1944 and 1956), it was Joyce's first novel. It was not, however, his first incursion into fiction. He had written a series of epiphanies (twenty-two in number) between 1901 and 1904, which did not, however, appear in print until 1956, though he had brought out *Dubliners*, a collection of short stories, in 1914. *A Portrait of the Artist* was followed by a play, *Exiles*, in 1918 and Joyce's second novel, *Ulysses*, in 1922. *Finnegans Wake*, Joyce's third novel, was published in 1939, *Chamber Music*, a sequence of thirty-six lyric poems, had appeared in 1907 and *Pomes Penyeach* in 1927.

Though I have referred throughout to the pagination of the Definitive Text of *A Portrait*, I have also given the chapter and section of the novel to enable readers with other editions to locate references.

1. The Subject

The title, *A Portrait of the Artist as a Young Man*, suggests a character study; nor is it surprising to find that the biographical subject-matter, which ranges from infancy to early manhood, illustrates development of character. The subject, however, is not so much the artist's relationships with other characters as his state of mind, the development of his attitudes. When, for example, Heron accuses Stephen of being no saint, we are told that:

> He [Stephen] scarcely resented what had seemed to him at first a silly indelicateness for he knew that the adventure in his mind stood in no danger from their words: and his face mirrored his rival's false smile. (II, iii, pp. 79–80)

Joyce's phrase, 'the adventure in his mind', well expresses the nature of the novel's subject-matter. The paramountcy of Stephen's subjective preoccupations and values in the face of external pressures and values is also very characteristic.

A Portrait might, therefore, be compared with a work like Wordsworth's *The Prelude*. So far as subject-matter is concerned, it does indeed belong to the kind of fiction known as the *Bildungsroman*, the novel of formation or education which describes the struggle from childhood towards maturity. Early examples include Goethe's *Wilhelm Meister*, Meredith's *The Ordeal of Richard Feverel*, Samuel Butler's *The Way of All Flesh* with all of which Joyce was familiar (see *Finnegans Wake*, Viking Press, 234, 621; *Ulysses*, Random House, 182, 197). Modern works of a similar kind include D. H. Lawrence's *Sons and Lovers*, Mann's *Magic Mountain*, Somerset Maugham's *Of Human Bondage*, Thomas Wolfe's *Look Homeward, Angel*. The subject common to all this fiction is that of a sensitive youth who is at first shaped by his environment but becomes conscious of its pressure and rebels against it to try to find his own identity or individuality. Unless the hero did not experience some measure of influence and shaping to begin with, his later rebellion would, of course, have little meaning, drama and power. It tends to follow that the rebellion is, in part, that of a son against father or mother/and against country, religion, and so on. Such novels tend also to spring from an autobiographical matrix, yet we should beware of treating them as fictionalized autobiography. For example, Stephen Dedalus is solemn but Joyce himself was witty and often gay. Unlike Stephen's father, Joyce's own father was not irresponsible. On the other hand, Joyce like Stephen appears to have been egocentric and introverted. It is hardly surprising that with such a subject characters may not exist in their own right but may be related and subordinated to the hero's development. Certainly, in *A Portrait of the Artist* not only the characters but also the structure, viewpoint and style are rigorously harnessed to the single task of displaying Stephen's character and its development.

2. *The Theme*

The theme of *A Portrait of the Artist* might be stated somewhat as follows. An artist is essentially an individual who can flourish only by becoming free of all collective entanglements and commitments in the external world. I do not think we should be sidetracked into such issues as whether, on the evidence of the villanelle, we consider Stephen a promising artist or not, or indeed into the subsequent history of Stephen in *Ulysses*. Joyce is simply laying down the minimum conditions for the survival of the will to art. As Stephen himself puts it to Davin, the nationalist:

> The soul is born, he said vaguely, first in those moments I told you of. It has a slow and dark birth, more mysterious than the birth of the body. When the soul of a man is born in this country there are nets flung at it to hold it back from flight. You talk to me of nationality, language, religion. I shall try to fly by those nets. (V, i, p. 207)

Later Cranly recapitulates Stephen's mature aim in life as:

> To discover the mode of life or of art whereby your spirit could express itself in unfettered freedom.
> Stephen raised his hat in acknowledgment. (V, iii, p. 250)

And Stephen tells Cranly:

> I will not serve that in which I no longer believe whether it call itself my home, my fatherland or my church: and I will try to express myself in some mode of life or art as freely as I can and as wholly as I can, using for my defence the only arms I allow myself to use—silence, exile, and cunning. (V, iii, p. 251)

Yet we should note that this specific theme concerning the artist does involve another and more general theme which closely concerns us all, the whole question of—indeed, the conflict and choice between—the collective and the individual life.

3. Structure

Since Joyce's subject is biographical, verisimilitude (or rather Joyce's concept of verisimilitude) demands that the subject be treated in a realistic vein. So far as construction is concerned, this means that events *are* be related in more or less chronological sequence, that is from infancy, through boyhood and adolescence, to early manhood; since the subject is also concerned with development, the natural order of growth should be imitated. Thus artificial structure should not be resorted to. Furthermore, since the biography deals with extremely subjective material (I leave aside Joyce's *objective handling* of this material), there is a strong temptation to realize the material in a lyrical rather than a dramatic manner. Art, however, as distinct from straight reporting from life, requires both selection and heightening to indicate and stress significance.

Joyce solves the structural problem posed by his avoidance of artificial structure in two ways. First, the subjective nature of his material—the revelation of Stephen's state of mind—enables Joyce to break chronological sequence in a natural manner, that is through the association of ideas which a narrative using even a limited form of 'stream-of-consciousness' makes possible. Thus, we can have 'flashbacks' which are significant yet seem natural. For example, Heron's banter and the cut of his cane against Stephen's leg together with the key word, 'admit' (here, that Stephen 'can't play the saint on me any more'), recalls an earlier episode involving Heron. A master had detected heresy in Stephen's essay, thereby injuring Stephen's self-esteem, and a few nights after 'this public chiding', Stephen is taunted by Heron and two other boys who try to beat Stephen into admitting that Byron was 'no good'. The episode juxtaposes the strength of Stephen's non-conformism and his inability to sustain anger or hatred (II, iii, pp. 80–84). The skilful join is managed thus:

> The confession came only from Stephen's lips and, while they spoke the words, a sudden memory had carried him to another scene called up, as if by magic, at the moment when he had noted the faint cruel dimples at the corners of Heron's smiling lips and had felt the familiar stroke of the cane against his calf and had heard the familiar word of admonition:
> —Admit. (II, iii, p. 80)

Secondly, Joyce avoids an artificial structure yet solves the problem of selection and heightening of effect through the use of epiphanies which indicate and stress significance.

In *Stephen Hero*, Joyce has Stephen define epiphany as 'a sudden spiritual manifestation'. We are told that the commonest, most trivial objects are capable of epiphany. Epiphany is identical with 'radiance' in the aesthetic theory Stephen expounds to Cranly in *Stephen Hero* and to Lynch in *A Portrait of the Artist*. When we have perceived the 'wholeness' (unity) of an object and the harmonious relation of its parts, the final stage in aesthetic apperception is radiance:

> We recognise that it is *that* thing which it is. Its soul, its whatness, leaps to us from the vestment of its appearance. The soul of the commonest object, the structure of which is so adjusted, seems to us radiant. The object achieves its epiphany. (*Stephen Hero*, 210–12, 213; cf. *A Portrait*, V, i, pp. 216–17)

We should perhaps also note that an ecclesiastical term is being secularized here. The feast of the Epiphany (6 January) celebrates the three kings (wise men) who saw a baby in a manger yet recognized more than a baby![1] William York Tindall, *A Reader's Guide to James Joyce* (London, 1959), p. 11, argues that epiphany equals symbolism and the radiant object a symbol. But the most important thing about epiphany is its

[1] The Greek word = 'a showing forth'; = revelation of what is concealed.

profound significance and I would myself consider the radiant object to
be extremely close to what we have come to call the *archetype* or *archetypal image*, since symbols may be personal and fail to communicate.
Epiphany as a process would thus resemble the constellation of archetypes
or archetypal symbols in the collective unconscious, their bringing forth
into consciousness, their amplification, and their being made meaningful
in the context of a personal life.

Much of Stephen's spiritual development, almost all its positive side
which tends towards aesthetic fulfilment is conveyed through epiphanies.
These provide lyrical moments of great power and significance, and often
of great beauty also. From a structural point of view, epiphanies provide
the climaxes of Stephen's progress, that is they mark the crises in what
we would call in a more conventional novel the plot—here the line of
inner action or internal drama.

For example, the second section of Chapter I, concludes with Stephen's
dream of Parnell's death which immediately follows Stephen's daydream
about his own death as a result of being pushed into the ditch by Wells
and suggests that self-pity reveals or finds relief in a kind of megalomania (I, ii, pp. 24, 27). Again, the first section of Chapter II ends with
Stephen's daydream about Mercedes (from Dumas' *The Count of Monte
Christo*) which expresses an early romantic form of woman's image (the
anima or bearer of the man's soul-image) in the adolescent boy. Stephen
intuits that when the image is projected on to a real woman this will
prove a transfiguring experience: 'then in a moment, he would be transfigured. Weakness and timidity and inexperience would fall from him
in that magic moment' (II, i, pp. 66–7). A good deal of the novel has to
do with Stephen's learning to interpret this intuition correctly: from his
experience of E.C. to his encounter with the prostitute and with the
wading girl. Thus, the episode between Stephen and E.C. at the tram
illustrates a conflict between Stephen's wish to go on projecting the
woman-image (or *anima*) as a romantic experience and a desire to realize
his developing sex urge which is breaking through the romantic image:

> His heart danced upon her movements like a cork upon a tide. He
> heard what her eyes said to him from beneath their cowl and knew that
> in some dim past, whether in life or in revery, he had heard their tale
> before. He saw her urge her vanities, her fine dress and sash and long
> black stockings, and knew that he had yielded to them a thousand
> times. Yet a voice within him spoke above the noise of his dancing
> heart, asking him would he take her gift to which he had only to
> stretch out his hand. . . .

—She too wants me to catch hold of her, he thought. That's why she came with me to the tram. I could easily catch hold of her when she comes up to my step: nobody is looking. I could hold her and kiss her.

But he did neither. (II, ii, pp. 71–2)

A series of epiphanies outline Stephen's painful, growing awareness of his alienation from family and society. Thus, the third section of Chapter II concludes with Stephen's evading his family after the Whitsuntide play at Belvedere and his distancing himself from his 'wounded pride', 'fallen hope', 'baffled desire', by inhaling the stench of the stables (II, iii, p. 89). When his father searches for his initials in the anatomy theatre at Queen's College, the sudden discovery of the word, 'Foetus', cut in a desk, shocks Stephen into an awareness of other obscene life reflecting his own 'monstrous reveries' (II, iv, pp. 92–3). Stephen finds in the moon a symbol of his cold and distant attitude towards human relationships, yet Shelley's lines on the moon with their cosmic vision raise Stephen above his own grief at his alienation (II, iv, pp. 98–9).

A further series of epiphanies trace the growth of Stephen's awareness of his state of mortal sin in Chapter III. Thus, Stephen finds an adequate expression of his cold sinful pride in the equation on his exercise book which comes to resemble a peacock's tail and a galaxy being born and dying. The peacock is, of course, a traditional emblem of pride, the equation suggests the intellect, abstract reason, and the cosmic scale may indicate the enormity of Stephen's sin in his own eyes and is certainly connected with the Lucifer motif in the novel and Stephen's sense of alienation (III, i, p. 106).

Again, Stephen's vision of his own particular hell and damnation, which follows Father Arnall's sermons, is an epiphany of terrifying power. In his plan for *Stephen Hero*, Joyce refers to this vision as 'Epiphany of Hell' (*The Workshop of Daedalus*, ed. R. Scholes and R. M. Kain, p. 69) and an earlier version of a dream-epiphany of hell is recorded by Joyce in his collection of epiphanies:

A field of stiff weeds and thistles and tufted nettlebunches. Thick among the tufts of rank stiff growth lay battered canisters and clots and coils of solid excrement. A faint marshlight struggled upwards from all the	A small field of still weeds and thistles alive with

ordure through the bristling greygreen weeds. An evil smell, faint and foul as the light, curled upwards sluggishly out of the canisters and from the stale crusted dung.

Creatures were in the field; one, three, six: creatures were moving in the field, hither and thither. Goatish creatures with human faces, hornybrowed, lightly bearded and grey as indiarubber. The malice of evil glittered in their hard eyes, as they moved hither and thither, trailing their long tails behind them. A rictus of cruel malignity lit up greyly their old bony faces. One was clasping about his ribs a torn flannel waistcoat, another complained monotonously as his beard stuck in the tufted weeds. Soft language issued from their spittleless lips as they swished in slow circles round and round the field, winding hither and thither through the weeds, dragging their long tails amid the rattling canisters. They moved in slow circles, circling closer and closer to enclose, to enclose, soft language issuing from their lips, their long swishing tails besmeared with stale shite, thrusting upwards their terrific faces . . . .

Help!

He flung the blankets from him madly to free his face and neck. That was his hell. God had allowed him to see the hell reserved for his sins: stinking,

confused forms, half-men, half-goats. Dragging their great tails they move thither and thither aggressively. Their faces are lightly bearded, pointed and grey as indiarubber. A secret personal sin directs them now, as in reaction, to constant malevolence. One is clasping about his body a torn flannel jacket; another complains monotonously as his beard catches in the stiff weeds.

They move about me, enclosing me, that old sin sharpening their eyes to cruelty, swishing through the fields in slow circles, thrusting upwards their terrific faces. Help! (MS. at Cornell; cited in *The Workshop of Daedalus*, p. 16)

bestial, malignant, a hell of
lecherous goatish fiends. For
him! For him! (III, iii, p. 141)

In Joyce's development of the earlier version of this epiphany, we can see a significant structural thinking at work. For what he adds in the novel to the indications of lust is essentially the excrement and the evil smell that link this vision of personal damnation not only with the almost cloacal strench and decay in Father Arnall's description of hell, but also with the sense of filth and degradation with which Stephen, in his lust, has come to associate the image of woman, and ultimately with the liberation of that image from filth and degradation in his aesthetic and spiritual perception of the wading girl.

Stephen's vision of damnation occurs in the third section of Chapter III and its placing is structurally significant. There is a careful symmetry about the design of Chapters III and IV which suggests they are to be taken as parallels—compared, that is, and, as we shall see, sharply contrasted. Chapter III might well be entitled, 'Sin', Chapter IV, 'Salvation'; the contrast is not a simple one but a complex, ironic one. Chapter III, Section i, shows Stephen's growing awareness of his state of mortal sin; Chapter IV, Section i, describes the apparent, orthodox amendment in Stephen's life (following his confession). Chapter III, Section ii, contains Father Arnall's terrifying sermons on the physical and spiritual torments of Hell (which help to prompt Stephen's confession); Chapter IV, Section ii, relates how Stephen hears but rejects the call to the priesthood (as a Jesuit). Chapter III, Section iii, describes Stephen's vision of damnation and his confession; Chapter IV, Section iii, describes how Stephen is liberated and reborn (outside a specific religious context) and discovers his true destiny and vocation as artist.

The whole of this third final section of Chapter IV is devoted to a series of epiphanies through which the climax of the novel and the turning-point in Stephen's spiritual development is superbly expressed. To begin with, Stephen's meeting with the Christian Brothers on the bridge at Dollymount is a finely executed piece of *transitus* symbolism. Stephen, who has just refused to accept the call to the priesthood, in spite of the appeal it makes to his pride and power-seeking, now finds himself going across a dividing line (the water) in the opposite direction to a group of priests. Stephen is alone, the priests are a squad marching together. That is, Stephen progresses towards individuality, the priests towards a collective life. Even so, Stephen acknowledges that the priests, who are not Jesuits but a lowly order, are truly devout, generous, humble and compassionate while Stephen lacks all these qualities. That is, Joyce does not represent Stephen's decision to reject the Church as a melodramatic choice (IV, iii, pp. 169–70). That the *transitus* symbolism here does indicate a decision can be seen if we glance back to the second sentence of the section in which Stephen hesitates between 'Byron's public house' (poetry and a secular life) and 'Clontorf Chapel' (nation—scene of Irish victory—and religion) (p. 168).

When Stephen encounters the bathers, the immersion symbolism is introduced—though in a comic manner ('Duck him', p. 172)—and the collective character of the bathers is used to heighten, by contrast, Stephen's individuality yet sense of isolation:

> He recognised their speech collectively before he distinguished their faces. . . . How characterless they looked. . . . Perhaps they had taken refuge in number and noise from the secret dread in their souls. But he, apart from them and in silence, remembered in what dread he stood of the mystery of his own body. (IV, iii, pp. 172–3)

Sensuality is muted as Stephen observes the chilly, 'repellent' and 'pitiable' quality of the bathers' wet adolescent nakedness.

What might be described as a 'Reconciling Symbol' begins to appear when the Daedalus and Icarus archetypes are constellated in Stephen. First, Stephen's egocentric pride and megalomania is transcended through the archetypal images:

> Their banter [that of the bathers] was not new to him and now it flattered his mild proud sovereignty. Now, as never before, his strange name seemed to him a prophecy. So timeless seemed the grey warm air, so fluid and impersonal his own mood, that all ages were as one to him. (IV, iii, p. 173)

True, Joyce never refers specifically to Icarus, an archetype of overweening pride, as he certainly does to Daedalus, the 'fabulous artificer', yet Joyce must surely have been well aware in the myth he adopted of the possibility of a complex figure in the 'hawklike man flying sunward', a potential for disaster as well as achievement and fulfilment which is perhaps just hinted at here in the word, 'sunward', but a problem transcended on this occasion, for Stephen soars on the wings of a purified pride, of genuine artistic aspiration, and is no longer inflated and sustained by egomania. He has become identified, that is, with Daedalus, the soaring craftsman-artist, where he might have fallen as Icarus, the proud son, whose wings were melted in his vainglorious flight too near the sun. In other words, Stephen escapes from the confines of the ego through identity with the archetype of the Self as craftsman-artist:

> Now, at the name of the fabulous artificer, he seemed to hear the noise of dim waves and to see a winged form flying above the waves and slowly climbing the air. What did it mean? Was it a quaint device opening a page of some medieval book of prophecies and symbols, a hawklike man flying sunward above the sea, a prophecy of the end he had been born to serve and had been following through the mists of childhood and boyhood, a symbol of the artist forging anew in his workshop out of the sluggish matter of the earth a new soaring impalpable imperishable being? (IV, iii, p. 173)

Stephen's experience of the archetype is an authentic one. In his elation he feels that he is soaring with Daedalus, that he is purified and become spirit:

> His heart trembled; his breath came faster and a wild spirit passed over his limbs as though he were soaring sunward. His heart trembled in an ecstasy of fear and his soul was in flight. His soul was soaring in an air beyond the world and the body he knew was purified in a breath and delivered of incertitude and made radiant and com-mingled with the element of the spirit. An ecstasy of flight made radiant his eyes and wild his breath and tremulous and wild and radiant his windswept limbs. (IV, iii, p. 173)

The experience also expresses a sense of liberation, 'His throat ached with a desire to cry aloud, the cry of a hawk or eagle on high, to cry piercingly of his deliverance to the winds' (IV, iii, p. 174), while the call to a true vocation is contrasted with other false calls:

> This was the call of life to his soul not the dull gross voice of the world of duties and despair, not the inhuman voice that had called him to the pale service of the altar. An instant of wild flight had delivered him and the cry of triumph which his lips withheld cleft his brain. (IV, iii, p. 174)

Furthermore, this experience is a genuine rebirth into new life from a state of spiritual deadness as well as a liberation into a creative attitude:

What were they now but cerements shaken from the body of death
—the fear he had walked in night and day, the incertitude that had
ringed him round, the shame that had abused him within and without
—cerements, the linens of the grave?

His soul had arisen from the grave of boyhood, spurning her graveclothes. Yes! Yes! Yes! He would create proudly out of the freedom
and power of his soul, as the great artificer whose name he bore, a
living thing, new and soaring and beautiful, impalpable, imperishable.
(IV, iii, p. 174)

There follows an urge towards expansion and discovery, 'a lust of
wandering in his feet that burned to set out for the ends of the earth . . .
dawn [would] . . . show him strange fields and hills and faces', and turning
to explore with the cry, 'Where?', Stephen confronts the sea, the
Unconscious if you like—or, if you prefer, the Ground or Source of our
Being.

Significantly, it is the turn of the tide (p. 174) and Stephen now joins
other figures who are immersing themselves. Baptism as a form of rebirth
suggests itself:

> . . . amid the shallow currents of the beach were lightclad gayclad
> figures, wading and delving.
> In a few moments he was barefoot, his stockings folded in his
> pockets and his canvas shoes dangling by their knotted laces over his
> shoulders and, picking a pointed salteaten stick out of the jetsam among
> the rocks, he clambered down the slope of the breakwater. (IV, iii,
> pp. 174–5)

Significantly again, Stephen retraces the water towards its source, an act
characteristic of introversion (or the backflowing of energy towards the
Unconscious) in the creative or individuation process: 'There was a long
rivulet in the strand and, as he waded slowly up its course, he wondered
at the endless drift of seaweed' (IV, iii, p. 175). This backflowing of
energy towards the Ground of Being in mystical experience usually
precedes a renewal of life and, sure enough, Stephen experiences a
renewal of life: 'a new wild life was singing in his veins' (p. 175). The
experience is also an initiation into manhood. It constitutes the loss of an
old identity and the birth of a new personality:

> Where was his boyhood now? Where was the soul that had hung
> back from her destiny, to brood alone upon the shame of her wounds
> and in her house of squalor and subterfuge to queen it in faded

cerements and in wreaths that withered at the touch? Or where was he? (IV, iii, p. 175)

Finally, the new personality will be one of positive individuality, for Stephen's sense of isolation is now a joyful one, in touch with life:

> He was alone. He was unheeded, happy and near to the wild heart of life. He was alone and young and wilful and wildhearted, alone amid a waste of wild air and brackish waters and the seaharvest of shells and tangle and veiled grey sunlight and gayclad lightclad figures of children and girls and voices childish and girlish in the air (IV, iii, p. 175)

Stephen now encounters the wading girl. The sheer lyrical power of this episode proclaims it to be the climax of the spiritual development which has been taking place within him. The obvious importance of the episode invites comparison and contrast with an earlier epiphany, the vision of hell and damnation in Chapter III, Section iii. It is significant that, at this stage in Stephen's spiritual progress, all that has gone before will be recapitulated in an archetypal image and that this should be the archetypal image of woman. What has been born, or brought to consciousness, is Stephen's soul and certain forms of the image of woman in man's imagination are familiar as the bearer of his soul (or *anima*). That the wading girl is a projection of something within Stephen is suggested by the fact that she too is alone and is wading like him, and is at the same time likened to a creature which can fly:

> A girl stood before him in midstream, alone and still, gazing out to sea. She seemed like one whom magic had changed into the likeness of a strange and beautiful seabird. (IV, iii, p. 175)

It is worth noting that in many mythologies, ancient Egyptian, for example, and much folklore (see Frazer's *The Golden Bough*), the soul is often conceived of as a bird, but this girl is a creature of the sea as well as of the air:

> Her long slender bare legs were delicate as a crane's and pure save where an emerald trail of seaweed had fashioned itself as a sign upon the flesh (IV, iii, p. 175)

She, therefore, suggests a figure emanating from the Collective Unconscious or Ground of Being (the ocean) and also a union of opposites. Such a union of air and water might indicate the union of intellect and feeling within Stephen. As a creature of the air, the girl also expresses a form of the Daedalus archetype, that is (in Joyce's terms) she represents freedom and the soaring experience associated with artistic inspiration and spiritual elation:

> Her bosom was as a bird's soft and slight, slight and soft as the breast of some darkplumaged dove. But her long fair hair was girlish. . . .
> —Heavenly God! cried Stephen's soul, in an outburst of profane joy. (IV, iii, pp. 175–6)

We might recall Stephen's earlier identification with a creature of the air, 'his soul was in flight. His soul was soaring in an air beyond the world' (p. 173).

As the bearer of Stephen's soul-image (*anima*-figure), the girl characteristically appears as if touched by magic: 'one whom magic had changed', we are told (IV, iii, p. 175). Although an obvious projection of Stephen in so many ways, her essentially feminine qualities indicate the *anima*-archetype, that image of woman within man: 'and girlish, and touched with the wonder of mortal beauty, her face' (IV, iii, p. 175). Much more important as regards Stephen's personal situation, what might have been sexual references in another context are transmuted here into something which bears an a-sexual, that is a non-sensual, connotation. It is interesting to see how this is done, how the obvious sexual images are immediately qualified by images which check all sensuality in the previous reference:

> Her long slender bare legs were delicate as a crane's and pure save where an emerald trail of seaweed had fashioned itself as a sign upon the flesh. Her thighs, fuller and softhued as ivory, were bared almost to the hips where the white fringes of her drawers were like featherings of soft white down. Her slateblue skirts were kilted boldly about her waist and dovetailed behind her. Her bosom was as a bird's soft and slight, slight and soft as the breast of some darkplumaged dove . . . her eyes turned to him in quiet sufferance of his gaze, without shame or wantonness. (IV, iii, pp. 175–6)

Thus, the girl's legs are 'long slender' and 'bare' yet 'delicate as a crane's', her thighs are 'fuller' and 'bared almost to the hips' yet 'softhued as ivory', 'the white fringes of her drawers' are glimpsed yet resemble 'featherings of soft white down', while her bosom is 'as a bird's soft and slight'. The emergence of an image of woman freed from a sensual context, yet transcending rather than denying that context, is an important development in Stephen since he had previously found the image of woman exciting either an adolescent romanticism or arousing lust, shame, guilt to a neurotic degree. To put the situation in another way, the soul-image (*anima*) has become the prisoner of his sexual urges, fantasies, and recriminations. His creative energy is locked up within a preoccupation with sex and sexual guilt. It is noteworthy that, earlier, feminine clothing had excited sexual thoughts in a fetishist way which anticipates one of Leopold Bloom's preoccupations in *Ulysses*. We are told that the adolescent Stephen saw E.C. 'urge her vanities, her fine dress and sash and long black stockings, and knew that he had yielded to them a thousand times' (II, ii, p. 71) and that later, for the young man, the

> names of articles of dress worn by women or of certain soft and delicate stuffs used in their making brought always to his mind a delicate and sinful perfume ... it was only amid softworded phrases or within rosesoft stuffs that he dared to conceive of the soul or body of a woman moving with tender life (IV, ii, pp. 158–9),

while the image of a woman's nude or semi-nude body had aroused masturbation fantasies:

> The sordid details of his orgies stank under his very nostrils: the sootcoated packet of pictures which he had hidden in the flue of the fireplace and in the presence of whose shameless or bashful wantonness he lay for hours sinning in thought and deed. (III, iii, p. 119)

We should also note the relationship between this aspect of the wading girl episode and Stephen's later definition of aesthetic emotion as 'static' ('The mind is arrested and raised above desire and loathing', V, i, p. 209)—while Lynch's mind dwells on 'the backside of the Venus of Praxiteles' (p. 209)—and we might well consider that Stephen's aesthetic theory expounded in Chapter V, Section i, is an intellectual reformulation of his experience of the wading girl.

Finally, the transformed image of woman is a kind of muse which summons Stephen to his secular vocation as a creator of art. Like a muse, she inspires him and clearly she becomes the bearer of his soul-image:

> Her image had passed into his soul for ever and no word had broken the holy silence of his ecstasy. Her eyes had called him and his soul had leaped at the call. To live, to err, to fall, to triumph, to recreate

life out of life! A wild angel had appeared to him, the angel of mortal youth and beauty, an envoy from the fair courts of life, to throw open before him in an instant of ecstasy the gates of all the ways of error and glory. (IV, iii, p. 176)

Significantly, the tide nears the turn (IV, iii, p. 196) and Stephen's vision becomes one of cosmic peace:

He felt above him the vast indifferent dome and the calm processes of the heavenly bodies; and the earth beneath him, the earth that had borne him, had taken him to her breast. (IV, iii, p. 176)

The cosmic vision takes in the awareness of a new world, a reminder that a change in attitude to the world means, in effect, the creation of a new world:

His eyelids trembled as if they felt the vast cyclic movement of the earth and her watchers, trembled as if they felt the strange light of some new world. His soul was swooning into some new world, fantastic, dim, uncertain as under sea, traversed by cloudy shapes and beings. (IV, iii, pp. 176–7)

Aptly, the concluding stage of Stephen's spiritual development in this section of the novel is symbolized by a flower of light which is on the cosmic scale: 'A world, a glimmer, or a flower.' The flower suggests fruition, the light spiritual illumination. But the flower, as a form of what we have come to call the *Mandala*, also suggests completeness: as does its equation with 'a world' and its cosmic nature:

Glimmering and trembling, trembling and unfolding, a breaking light, an opening flower, it spread in endless succession to itself, breaking in full crimson and unfolding and fading to palest rose, leaf by leaf and wave of light by wave of light, flooding all the heavens with its soft flushes, every flush deeper than other. (IV, iii, p. 177)

A final series of epiphanies in Chapter V expresses Stephen's attempts to realize his vocation as artist. Thus, we are given Stephen's vision of creative inspiration which issues in the villanelle (V, ii, pp. 221–3) and the act of poetic creation is seen as a kind of mass: 'a priest of eternal imagination, transmuting the daily bread of experience into the radiant body of everliving life. The radiant image of the eucharist . . .' (V, ii, p. 225). I personally think that surprise at Stephen's secular use of religious terms or vague talk about his clinging to the church he is rejecting misses the whole point of the novel. It depreciates the essentially *spiritual* nature of Stephen's progress towards an identity, a self-realization as artist. Spirituality and the aesthetic experience are not set up as an antithesis in the book. What Joyce is saying is that it is a false spirituality which denies the claims of the flesh (in the wrong way) for it thus denies life itself. The vocation of artist, indeed, demands a renunciation of certain things—not an asceticism, as such, but a renunciation of more than the priest, perhaps, is called on to make. Not a rejection of the World, the Flesh, and the Devil, but of family, religion and nation. While watching the flight of birds, Stephen experiences the archetypes of Daedalus and Thoth, god of writers, and perceives that his vocation as an artist demands of him that final terrible form of isolation which we call Exile:

> And for ages men had gazed upward as he was gazing at birds in flight. The colonnade above him made him think vaguely of an ancient temple and the ashplant on which he leaned wearily of the curved stick of an augur. A sense of fear of the unknown moved in the heart of his weariness, a fear of symbols and portents, of the hawklike man whose name he bore soaring out of his captivity on osierwoven wings, of Thoth, the god of writers, writing with a reed upon a tablet and bearing on his narrow ibis head the cusped moon . . . he felt that the augury he had sought in the wheeling darting birds and in the pale space of sky above him had come forth from his heart like a bird from a turret quietly and swiftly.
>
> Symbol of departure or of loneliness? (V, iii, pp. 229–30)

Yet Stephen finally embraces his fate with elation and we certainly see in a clear repetition of an earlier experience, that is in the final development of the Daedalus archetype, confirmation that Stephen has, in finding a cultural task in life, progressed from identity with the ego to identity with the self; that is, as artist, he has transcended the ego and thus invokes the aid of the 'old artificer', symbol of the artistic Self:

> The spell of arms and voices: the white arms of roads, their promise of close embraces and the black arms of tall ships that stand against the moon, their tale of distant nations. They are held out to say: We are alone. Come. And the voices say with them: We are your kinsmen. And the air is thick with their company as they call to me, their kinsman, making ready to go, shaking the wings of their exultant and terrible youth. . . . Welcome, O life! I go to encounter for the millionth

time the reality of experience and to forge in the smith of my soul the uncreated conscience of my race. . . . Old father, old artificer, stand me now and ever in good stead. (V, iii, p. 257)

4. Characterization

Since Stephen's spiritual development is the subject of the novel, the characterization of Stephen obviously occupies a central position in the scheme of the book; yet this central position is not without some subtle significance when we reflect that one of Stephen's main traits of character is his egocentricity. Furthermore, other characters are ruthlessly subordinated, harnessed to the task of bringing out Stephen's character. Thus, Davin (the nationalist), Lynch, and Cranly are used to bring out Stephen's ideas about Ireland, the Church, aesthetics. Heron is used to bring out the strength of Stephen's non-conformism, and so on.[1] This is not to deny that, as in the case of Stephen's father, such subordinate characters may be extremely life-like.

The most important point to grasp about Stephen's character, in my view, is not his pride, not even his egocentricity, but his introverted

---

[1] Indeed, Professor Theodore Spencer, in his introduction to his edition of *Stephen Hero*, revised John J. Slocum and Herbert Cahoon (London, 1956), notes that this rigid subordination of minor characters to the task of bringing out Stephen's character is one of the differences between the earlier and later versions of the novel: 'He was aiming at economy, and he was trying to place his centre of action as much as possible inside the consciousness of his hero. . . . For example: in the *Portrait* we are introduced to Stephen's friends—Cranly, Lynch and the rest—as items, so to speak, in Stephen's mind. They are not pictured for us; Joyce expects us to take them for granted, as features in Stephen's landscape which need no further identification beyond their names and their way of speaking. But in the present text [*Stephen Hero*] . . . they leave an independent reality of their own, like the people in *Dubliners*; they are not merely sounding boxes or slot-machines, as they are in the *Portrait*, for the ideas of the all-important Stephen.' Cf. Richard Ellmann, *James Joyce* (New York, 1959), p. 308: '. . . other human beings are not allowed much existence except as influences upon the soul's development or features of it. The same figures appear and reappear, the schoolboy Heron, for example, each time in an altered way to suggest growth in the soul's view of them.'

temperament. He belongs to what has been called (by C. G. Jung) the introverted thinking type. It is also perhaps worth noting that case-histories of this character-type show that his egocentricity is liable to deteriorate into power-seeking, megalomania, and other forms of egomania. On the other hand, a psychological process known as 'individuation' or the 'integration of the personality' is strikingly similar in its general pattern to that of Stephen's later development.

Stephen's introverted temperament is clearly indicated in the picture of his early childhood; thus during a football session at school:

> He kept on the fringe of his line, out of sight of his prefect, out of the reach of the rude feet, feigning to run now and then. He felt his body small and weak amid the throng of players and his eyes were weak and watery. (I, ii, p. 8)

We note that Stephen feels himself to be an outsider. He is withdrawn, introspective, sensitive, and on the defensive—resorting to cunning tactics to cover up his weak position and avoid commitment. This early account should certainly be compared with Stephen's final, mature statement of his position, as 'using for my defence . . . silence, exile, and cunning' (V, iii, p. 251), at the end of the novel. We also note quite early that introverted tendency to try to realize a subjective vision in the external world: 'But you could not have a green rose. But perhaps somewhere in the world you could' (I, ii, p. 12). And, as an adolescent, we really see him begin to resist the claims of the external world, setting up his own subjective values and interests against the values and interests of social institutions:

> While his mind had been pursuing its intangible phantoms and turning in irresolution from such pursuit he had heard about him the constant voices of his father and of his masters, urging him to be a gentleman above all things and urging him to be a good catholic above all things. These voices had now come to be hollow-sounding in his ears. When the gymnasium had been opened he had heard another voice urging him to be strong and manly and healthy and when the movement towards national revival had begun to be felt in the college yet another voice had bidden him be true to his country and help to raise up her fallen language and tradition. In the profane world, as he foresaw, a worldly voice would bid him raise up his father's fallen state by his labours and, meanwhile, the voice of his school comrades urged him to be a decent fellow, to shield others from blame or to beg them off and to do his best to get free days for the

school. And it was the din of all these hollowsounding voices that made him halt irresolutely in the pursuit of phantoms. He gave them ear only for a time but he was happy only when he was far from them, beyond their call, alone or in the company of phantasmal comrades. (II, iii, pp. 86-7)

As an adult, Stephen's introverted temperament expresses itself in a more sophisticated and (we may consider) a more constructive manner. It provides the basis of his aesthetic attitude:

> ... was it that, being as weak of sight as he was shy of mind, he drew less pleasure from the reflection of the glowing sensible world through the prism of a language manycoloured and richly storied than from the contemplation of an inner world of individual emotions mirrored perfectly in a lucid supple periodic prose? (IV, iii, p. 171)

Again, introversion in the adult Stephen is the basis of a more meaningful defensiveness but one which uses a more highly developed form of the very weapons he had used as a child:

> I will not serve that in which I no longer believe whether it call itself my home, my fatherland or my church: and I will try to express myself in some mode of life or art as freely as I can and as wholly as I can, using for my defence the only arms I allow myself to use—silence, exile, and cunning. (V, iii, p. 251)

It is worth noting here that Stephen's isolation, his alienation from family, school, religion, nation, which finally culminates in voluntary exile, is, at all stages, a logical conclusion of his fundamental introverted attitude (I, ii, p. 8; II, iv, pp. 94-5; II, v, p. 101; V, i, p. 207; V, iii, p. 251). Stephen can seek and find his own identity, his individuality, only by resisting all collective relationships, that is through isolation. Through a withdrawal which becomes more positive in its aim as he matures.

Stephen's egocentricity also derives from his introverted attitude. This egocentricity certainly has its negative aspect; from it issue what we would condemn as various manifestations of pride. Significantly, the section which sketches Stephen's early infancy concludes with an episode in which Stephen is defiant: 'He hid under the table. His mother said: —O, Stephen will apologize. Dante said: —O, if not, the eagles will come and pull out his eyes' (I, i, p. 8). Again, when Wells pushes Stephen into the ditch and Stephen becomes ill, his pride and self-pity find expression in a daydream of his own death and funeral whereby he gets his own back on Wells: 'And Wells would be sorry then for what he had done' (I, ii, p. 24). Characteristically, Stephen's reaction to the unjust punishment administered by Father Dolan is a sense of injured merit:

> Then to be called a schemer before the class and to be pandied when he always got the card for first or second and was the leader of the Yorkists! . . . It was cruel and unfair to make him kneel in the middle of the class then: and Father Arnall had told them both [Stephen and Fleming, the idler] that they might return to their places without making any difference between them. (I, iv, p. 53)

Stephen finds both pleasure ('he began to taste the joy of his loneliness' (II, ii, p. 70)) and a sense of superiority in his isolation:

> The noise of children at play annoyed him and their silly voices made him feel, even more keenly than he had felt at Clongowes, that he was different from others. (II, i, p. 66)

There are also distinct signs of megalomania in Stephen. When he is unjustly punished at school, for example, he seizes on a historical precedent which has the effect of focusing an adult critical attention on the boy's inflated, if naïve, sense of self-importance:

> He would go up and tell the rector that he had been wrongly punished. A thing like that had been done before by somebody in history, by some great person whose head was in the books of history. And the rector would declare that he had been wrongly punished because the senate and the Roman people always declared that the men who did that had been wrongly punished. (I, iv, pp. 54-5)

Later, the adolescent Stephen identifies himself with Napoleon:

> Stephen, who had read of Napoleon's plain style of dress, chose to remain unadorned and thereby heightened for himself the pleasure of taking counsel with his lieutenant before giving orders. (II, i, p. 65)

As an adult, we find Stephen identifying himself with St Stephen ('crossing Stephen's, that is, my green', V, iv, p. 253), with Jesus (Cranly is his John the Baptist, V, iv, p. 252), with Lucifer. Echoing Lucifer's *non serviam* in Father Arnall's sermon, Stephen declares, 'I will not serve that in which I no longer believe' (III, ii, p. 121; V, iii, p. 251). Nevertheless, Stephen's rebellion in the book is seen as a positive act and it rather looks as if this rebellion required so great an effort on his part that he needed to identify himself with all the energy which the great archetypal rebel appears to release in us when he takes hold of our imagination. One thinks, of course, of Milton's Satan and of Blake's insight into this condition.

> To live [writes Joyce], to err, to fall, to triumph, to recreate life out of life! A wild angel had appeared to him, the angel of mortal youth and beauty, an envoy from the fair courts of life, to throw open before him in an instant of ecstasy the gates of all the ways of error and glory. (IV, iii, p. 176)

Similarly, Stephen makes something constructive out of what, in another context, would have been a blasphemous megalomania when be sees himself as godlike in his creativity and objectivity as an artist:

> The artist, like the God of the creation, remains within or behind or beyond or above his handiwork, invisible, refined out of existence, indifferent, paring his fingernails. (V, i, p. 219)

All the same, this detached attitude, which is extolled as an ideal for the artist, is shown in a very different light when it is adopted in real human relationships. A good deal earlier in the novel, we are shown that Stephen's egocentricity results in a lack of compassion, even sympathy (II, iv, p. 90), that he is unable to respond to any human appeal (II, iv, p. 95), and that he is cold and experiences not love but lust (II, iv, p. 98).

During his later adolescence, Stephen's view of his egocentricity and sexual appetite is in strict accordance with what he believes the Church's teaching about pride and lust to be. Joyce makes it clear that, with the coming of adolescence, Stephen's egocentricity finds its natural expression not in love but in lust (II, iv, p. 98; cf. II, v, pp. 101–2) and, in describing the agony of frustrated lust, Joyce makes its obscenity plain (II, v, pp. 102–3). Pride prevents Stephen's seeking absolution from what he clearly recognizes as a state of mortal sin and, following the Church's teaching, he acknowledges the interconnectedness of his lust and pride, indeed, of all sin (III, i, pp. 106–7, 109). One critic at least (Barbara Seward) has seen the wading girl episode as the complete deliverance of

Stephen from the restraints placed upon his sexuality by the Church. In my view, this is too facile an interpretation. Joyce was too intelligent and too well-schooled in reasoning by the Jesuits not to incorporate in his later view of things whatever he found of indisputable truth in the Church's teaching. This is the real sense in which Joyce, I think, can be said never to have left the Church. But where he does part company with the Church is in the *final* answer to the problem of Stephen's egocentricity and sexuality. To the problem of sexuality he finds, in the first place, not a moral but an aesthetic solution; not aesthetic, that is, in any superficial sense but in a truly spiritual, a quasi-religious sense (as we saw in analysing Stephen's encounter with the wading girl). In seeking an answer to the problem of Stephen's egocentricity, Joyce is comprehensive enough to take in certain positive aspects of egocentricity and daring enough to proclaim these as essential in the artist's development. It is difficult to see how Stephen could have found his true identity and his real vocation as artist and entered upon that vocation without, for example, the compulsion to excel which he exhibits at Belvedere in his essays (II, iii, pp. 80–81), without that defiant non-conformism whose strength he demonstrates in the encounter with Heron (II, iii, pp. 83–4), without the rebelliousness (I, i, p. 8; II, iii, pp. 80–81) which is no passing phase (II, iii, pp. 86–7) but so deep-seated as to result in Stephen's identification with the great rebel angel (IV, iii, p. 176; V, iii, p. 251), and without that ruthless pursuit of individuality which shatters the collective ties to family, nation, religion (V, i, p. 207; V, iii, p. 251). That Stephen's pride might have been dealt with satisfactorily within the Church may well be questioned by Joyce when he shows Stephen's pride to be much in evidence on the way to confess (III, iii, p. 144) and even after confession (IV, i, pp. 155–7). There is certainly a sly irony in the priest's appeal to Stephen to become a priest which is couched in terms that will appeal to his pride and desire for power:

A strong note of pride reinforcing the gravity of the priest's voice made Stephen's heart quicken in response.
—To receive that call, Stephen, said the priest, is the greatest honour that the Almighty God can bestow upon a man. No king or emperor on this earth has the power of the priest of God. No angel or archangel in heaven, no saint, not even the Blessed Virgin herself has the power of a priest of God: the power of the keys, the power to bind and to loose from sin, the power of exorcism, the power to cast out from the creatures of God the evil spirits that have power over them, the power, the authority, to make the great God of Heaven come down upon the

altar and take the form of bread and wine. What an awful power, Stephen!

A flame began to flutter again on Stephen's cheek as he heard in this proud address an echo of his own proud musings. (IV, ii, p. 161)

Since Stephen rejects this call to vanity and power any crude equation between Stephen's egocentricity and pride needs questioning. It is freedom not power which Stephen finally seeks:

> Then he wondered . . . at the frail hold which so many years of order and obedience had of him when once a definite and irrevocable act of his threatened to end for ever, in time and in eternity, his freedom. . . . The wisdom of the priest's appeal did not touch him to the quick. He was destined to learn his own wisdom apart from others or to learn the wisdom of others himself wandering among the snares of the world. (IV, ii, p. 165)

5. *Viewpoint*

The problem of viewpoint in *A Portrait of the Artist* arises from Joyce's attempt at objectivity. Stephen Dedalus describes extreme objectivity as the ideal attitude of the artist towards his subject:

> The personality of the artist, at first a cry or a cadence or a mood and then a fluid and lambent narrative, finally refines itself out of existence, impersonalises itself, so to speak. The esthetic image in the dramatic form is life purified in and reprojected from the human imagination. The mystery of esthetic like that of material creation is accomplished. The artist, like the God of the creation is accomplished. The artist, like the God of the creation, remains within or behind or beyond or above his handiwork, invisible, refined out of existence, indifferent, paring his fingernails. (V, i, p. 219)

Yet can the novelist stand aside from his novel so completely as this? Or does—or indeed should—the novelist give some pointer towards his own attitude, some indication of the attitude he wishes the reader to take up towards the subject of the novel, the characters, theme, and so on?

Certainly, in *A Portrait of the Artist*, the viewpoint is frequently Stephen's. Joyce even adapts his style to situation so as to convey Stephen's viewpoint more convincingly and more compellingly. Thus, the use of baby talk or schoolboy language in the early parts of the novel, with its concrete circumstantial detail, its stress on discovery and question-ing, and its apperception of the external world through sensuous experience brings Stephen's infancy and boyhood directly before us with marvellous exactness and living force:

. . . his father looked at him through a glass: he had a hairy face.
He was baby tuckoo. The moocow came down the road . . .
When you wet the bed, first it is warm then it gets cold. His mother put on the oil-sheet. That had the queer smell.
His mother had a nicer smell than his father (I, i, p. 7)

He leaned his elbows on the table and shut and opened the flaps of his ears. Then he heard the noise of the refectory every time he opened the flaps of his ears. It made a roar like a train at night. And when he closed the flaps the roar was shut off like a train going into a tunnel. (I, ii, p. 13)

—I wouldn't like to be Simon Moonan and Tusker, Cecil Thunder said. But I don't believe they will be flogged. Perhaps they will be sent up for twice nine.
—No, no, said Athy. They'll both get it on the vital spot. (I, iv, p. 45)

One problem with extreme objectivity in the novel is how to dis-tinguish between a character's viewpoint (especially the hero's) and what we might call the point of view of the novel as a whole. For example, how far are the point of view in *A Portrait of the Artist* and Stephen's viewpoint identical? Since Stephen has a vital change of heart during the course of the novel, how far can his viewpoint be relied upon? This is, of course, the problem of reliable and unreliable narrators which has come to the fore in recent years, largely through Wayne C. Booth's study of the problems in *The Rhetoric of Fiction* (Chicago, 1961).

What is more, for all Stephen's vaunted objectivity, Joyce does employ a rhetoric which indicates direction to the reader. When Stephen is a small boy at Clongowes, his megalomania and naïvety are exposed and deflated by what can only seem, on the part of so conscious an artist as Joyce, a deliberately chosen device. By means of the historical precedent, unwittingly grasped at by Stephen, an ironic discrepancy is established between Stephen's naïve view of his own predicament and the sophisticated reader's view of it, perhaps shared in some measure and even focused by the skittish 'fellows out of second of grammar':

> And there were some fellows out of second of grammar listening and one of them said:
> —The senate and the Roman people declared that Dedalus had been wrongly punished. . . .
> . . . He would go up and tell the rector that he had been wrongly punished. A thing like that had been done before by somebody in history, by some great person whose head was in the books of history. And the rector would declare that he had been wrongly punished because the senate and the Roman people always declared that the men who did that had been wrongly punished. (I, iv, 54–5)

If one argues that this is the dramatic objective method, then one should contrast the episode with the following examples. Thus, an ironic view of Stephen's bogus repentance is conveyed through absurdly inflated images which cast doubt on the genuineness of Stephen's attitude and prepare us for his change of heart later in the novel (IV, i, p. 151). Again, a form of bathos is used to comment on Stephen's false attitude (IV, i, p. 154).[1]

The crucial problem of *A Portrait of the Artist* is how we are to take Stephen's final attitude in the novel. This is where the objective method, the absence of a clear rhetoric hinders us. It should be noted that the novel need not imply that Stephen will be a successful artist. Whether the villanelle is a good or bad poem is, therefore, irrelevant and so is what happens to Stephen in *Ulysses*. It is enough that Joyce has laid down the conditions for the artist and that Stephen has found salvation in determining on the aesthetic rather than the social, nationalistic, or religious orientation in life. It has been argued that Joyce's whole attitude to Stephen's development is ironic. Yet, if we compare the authenticity of the experience on the Strand (IV, iii, pp. 168–77) with Stephen's bogus repentance (IV, i, pp. 148–57) or his rejection of the priesthood (IV, ii, pp. 157–68) with the powerful affirmation of his vocation as artist from Chapter IV, section iii, to the end of the book it is difficult not to take sides or to credit that Joyce himself was not on the side of the artist as a young man.[2] All this, of course, is not to deny the reality of Stephen's guilty feelings when he considers himself to be in a

[1] For a fuller discussion of these passages, see below, pp. 48–9.
[2] For further discussion on this point, see below, pp. 55–9.

state of mortal sin or to deny the power of Father Arnall's sermons (III, ii) which are directed at a Roman Catholic who has not lost his faith at that point in the novel.

6. Myth and Symbol

Like many other great works of art, *A Portrait of the Arist as a Young Man* is based upon a myth, a traditional archetypal pattern of heroes and events, which is treated, even elaborated, to accommodate the author's special meaning. Just as in *Ulysses*, Joyce relates his central characters and their stories in different ways, ironic and otherwise, to the personages and events described in Homer's *Odyssey*, so in *A Portrait of the Artist as a Young Man*, Joyce underscores the unity and meaning of his work by founding it upon the myth of Daedalus. So important did Joyce regard his reference to this myth that he carefully prefaced the novel with a quotation drawn from the original story in Ovid's *Metamorphoses* which might be translated, 'And he turned his mind to unknown arts.' The context of this quotation, in Golding's translation, is as follows:

> Now in this while 'gan Daedalus a weariness to take
> Of living like a banished man and prisoner such a time
> In Crete, and longed in his heart to see his native clime.
> But seas enclosed him as if he had in prison be.
> Then thought he: 'Though both sea and land King Minos stop
> from me,
> I am assured he cannot stop the air and open sky.
> To make my passage that way then my cunning will I try,
> Although that Minos like a lord held all the world beside:
> Yet doth the air from Minos' yoke for all men free abide.'
> This said: to uncouth [unknown] arts he bent the force of all his
> wits
> To alter Nature's course by craft. (VIII, ll. 245-55; spelling and
> capitalization modernized)

Like his namesake, the 'fabulous artificer', who builds himself wings, Stephen will also escape from the island prison which Ireland has become to him. And he will do this not only literally by going abroad but also spiritually by soaring on the wings of art into the air, that medium of intellect and inspiration. Yet the basic myth is more elaborate than this. On his fabulous flight, Daedalus took with him his son, Icarus, who in his youthful pride flew too near the sun so that the wax which held together his wings melted and he fell into the Aegean Sea where he was drowned. Icarus and his story are never specifically mentioned by Joyce in the novel but they are obviously there in the theme of Stephen's pride. Stephen, that is, embodies both Icarus and Daedalus and bears within him the potential fate of either. The conflict between pride and selfhood expresses, as we have seen, the central psychological and spiritual problem of the novel. And we should not forget that Stephen must necessarily be both Icarus and Daedalus since selfhood can grow only out of an initial egocentricity. In other words, Stephen must assert his independence of family, nation, and religion at the crudest level of development first. Though, as the novel shows us, this is not sufficient.

In naming his hero, however, Joyce refers also to the story of the first Christian martyr, St Stephen. The novelist draws our attention to this reference when his hero is crossing St Stephen's Green but the Christian story does not play so important a role in the novel as the pagan myth of Daedalus. Like St Stephen, the hero of *A Portrait of the Artist as a Young Man* is, or at least sees himself as, a martyr, a person whose potential spiritual dedication is thwarted by the Irish. But the reference is largely negative and it obviously relates to the self-pitying martyr-like posture of the first chapter of the novel, an aspect of Stephen's pride.

Enough has already been said to indicate the important role symbolism plays in *A Portrait of the Artist as a Young Man* but not enough perhaps to show its contribution to overall structure and unity. Certainly, the two most important symbolic clusters in the novel are those polarizing round water/immersion and bird/flight.

The water symbolism is treated in such a way as to bring out the potentiality for development and regression in fundamental life and feeling. From the bed-wetting in the fifth paragraph of the book and the 'cold and slimy' ditch into which Stephen is shouldered later in the chapter, water represents the condition from which Stephen must grow, both the state of stagnation, of fixation, of psychological and spiritual death into which he can fall back and the possibility of baptism, the element from which he can be reborn. This water symbolism continues to be developed with a subtle modulation throughout the novel, registering minor and major phases of advance and regression, the hot and cold water taps in the lavatory at Clongowes, the sound of the cricket bats after his apparent victory over Father Dolan 'like drops of water in a fountain falling softly in the brimming bowl' (I, iv, p. 30). The realistically squalid opening of the fifth chapter when Stephen 'drained his third cup of watery tea to the dregs' and stared 'into the dark pool of the jar' and found that the 'yellow dripping had been scooped out like a boghole and the pool under it brought back to his memory the dark turfcoloured water of the bath in Clongowes' (p. 177). It is, therefore, no accident that in the *transitus* episode at Dollymount where Stephen encounters the Christian Brothers, the bridge is laid across water to which Joyce draws our attention and that we are told: 'Angry with himself he tried to hide his face from their eyes by gazing down sideways into the shallow swirling water under the bridge but he still saw a reflection therein of their topheavy silk hats, and humble tapelike collars and loosely hanging clerical clothes' (IV, iii, p. 170). Nor is it accidental that Joyce particularly indicates the shallowness of the water in which the image of those who follow a collective religious fate is reflected. Again, it is not fortuitous that in Chapter IV the episode of the bathing boys almost immediately precedes that of the wading girl and that the great turning-point in Stephen's spiritual development is a *seaside* epiphany. The boys bathing in the sea, somewhat like the Christian Brothers, are immersed in the collective life, though here expressed in instinctive and social energy: 'He [Stephen] recognised their speech collectively. . . . How characterless they looked' (IV, iii, p. 172). And yet, all unwittingly, they summon Stephen to his conscious individual baptism, to the rebirth of his soul in the figure of the wading girl:

A voice from beyond the world was calling.
—Hello, Stephanos!
—Here comes The Dedalus! . . .
. . . Now, as never before, his strange name seemed to him a prophecy. . . .
. . . This was the call of life to his soul. . . .
. . . His soul had arisen from the grave of boyhood, spurning her graveclothes. (IV, iii, pp. 172–4)

All this is made clearer by contrast, for, like Icarus, the other boys are submerged in a collective experience which is death to the individual soul, and it is a mark of Joyce's genius that he renders the trivial commonplace and undramatic nature of this experience: '—O, cripes, I'm drownded!' (IV, iii, p. 173).

The wading girl is a hybrid creature. At one point she is described as a 'seabird' and at another point her legs are compared to 'a crane's'. Indeed, while she stands 'in midstream' with 'an emerald trail of seaweed . . . as a sign upon the flesh', her slender lightness, the reference to her 'featherings' and the colour of her 'slateblue skirts . . . kilted boldly about her waist and dovetailed behind her' (IV, iii, p. 175) all indicate the elements from which and into which she will presently soar. Here, the duality of Stephen's being is resolved through the union of the two major symbolic clusters of the novel, yet a page or so earlier they had still been seen in opposition, since conflict must precede resolution, differentiation must precede integration:

> Now, at the name of the fabulous artificer, he seemed to hear the noise of dim waves and to see a winged form flying above the waves and slowly climbing the air. What did it mean? Was it a quaint device opening a page of some medieval book of prophecies and symbols, a hawklike man flying sunward above the sea, a prophecy of the end he had been born to serve and had been following through the mists of childhood and boyhood, a symbol of the artist forging anew in his workshop out of the sluggish matter of the earth a new soaring impalpable imperishable being?
>
> . . . his soul was in flight. His soul was soaring in an air beyond the world. (IV, iii, p. 173)

It is, of course, at this point that symbol merges into the overt mythopoeic structure of the book and that we feel again the power of its organic unity.

7. *Language, Style and Vision*

James Joyce shows a versatility in using language unequalled in English fiction outside Dickens. Indeed, we might well regard him, along with Dickens, as one of the two greatest virtuosi in this respect in the history of the English novel. It is, therefore, hardly surprising to find the author of *Ulysses* and *Finnegans Wake* displaying a verbal dexterity of a masterly kind in his earlier novel, *A Portrait of the Artist as a Young Man*, though his display is not so obtrusive and audacious as in the two later works of fiction.

To say, as has often been said, that Joyce adjusts his style to suit his subject matter, is to convey a scarcely adequate notion of the wonderful skill with which he uses language to focus his vision and the effect this has on his achievement. Joyce, that is, does not merely employ an ornamental or ostentatious rhetoric: his style is committed wholly and profoundly to the artistic task in hand and his language invariably demonstrates a structural relevance and an aptness of texture which goes far towards explaining the clarity, precision, and power of his vision.

For example, in the first chapter of *A Portrait of the Artist as a Young Man*, Joyce renders the early home-life and education of his hero with an immediacy and authenticity quite unrivalled outside the early pages of Dickens's *David Copperfield* and *Great Expectations* or Charlotte Brontë's *Jane Eyre*. And the vehicle of this vision is a realism appropriately subjective or objective as the case demands. Thus, the inner world of the child, the world he perceives and his manner of perceiving it, is wonderfully recaptured not through the stream-of-consciousness technique proper but by means of what can only be described as subjective realism:

Once upon a time and a very good time it was there was a moocow coming down along the road and this moocow that was coming down along the road met a nicens little boy named baby tuckoo. . . .

His father told him that story: his father looked at him through a glass: he had a hairy face.

He was baby tuckoo. The moocow came down the road where Betty Byrne lived: she sold lemon platt.

> O, the wild rose blossoms
> On the little green place.

He sang that song. That was his song.

> O, the green wothe botheth.

When you wet the bed, first it is warm then it gets cold. His mother put on the oilsheet. That had the queer smell.

His mother had a nicer smell than his father. She played on the piano the sailor's hornpipe for him to dance. He danced:

> Tralala lala
> Tralala tralaladdy. (I, i, p. 7)

Language, as here, is largely restricted to that of the appropriate age level.

This is true of the choice of vocabulary with its short basic words and nursery expressions, mainly monosyllabic, the unsophisticated syntax of the opening multiple sentence with its repetitive conjunction, 'and', and its breathless lack of punctuation, and the short simple staccato sentences and brief uncomplicated paragraphs which follow. Such a style reinforces the realistic impression of the child's vision with its narrow and limited preoccupations and its direct and concrete manner of apprehending the external world through the senses, here, of sight, touch, hearing and smell. Yet this passage does not convey infant concerns only. In conveying Stephen's early interest in music, rhythm, poetry, story, biography, parents and identity, it also indicates potentiality and possibility, the direction Stephen will travel. While growth, the basic theme and structure of the novel, is also reflected in the language which moves from the wholly infantile to the forms of later childhood.

Similarly, growth is continued in subsequent sections of the chapter, when Stephen's early boyhood is presented through its preoccupations and feelings, its modes of perception and its appropriate language. There is, of course, the schoolboy slang, 'the fellows', 'who fecked it?', 'scut', 'smugging', 'wrote things for cod', 'sending us up for six and eight every minute', 'into a wax', 'waxy', 'pandied', 'a stinking mean low trick', 'Baldyhead Dolan', and so on, together with the attitudes and activities of small boys at school. But there is also the interior viewpoint of Stephen, his anxieties about an external world which impinges upon him, threatens him, and which he still perceives quite naïvely through his senses, sensations which can reach a painful degree of acuteness and render a world remarkably concrete and immediate:

> The fellows laughed; but he felt that they were a little afraid. In the silence of the soft grey air he heard the cricketbats from here and from there: pock. That was a sound to hear but if you were hit then you would feel a pain. The pandybat made a sound too but not like that. The fellows said it was made of whalebone and leather with lead inside: and he wondered what was the pain like. There were different kinds of pains for all the different kinds of sounds. A long thin cane would have a high whistling sound and he wondered what was that pain like. It made him shivery to think of it and cold: and what Athy said too. But what was there to laugh at in it? It made him shivery: but that was because you always felt like a shiver when you let down your trousers. It was the same in the bath when you undressed yourself. He wondered who had to let them down, the master or the boy himself. O how could they laugh about it in that way? (I, iv, p. 46)

LANGUAGE, STYLE, AND VISION 39

This passage is, of course, related structurally to the rest of the section since it develops the theme of corporal punishment that is to culminate in Stephen's being unjustly pandied by Father Dolan. Indeed, the passage helps to prepare for that incident, which will prompt Stephen's visit to the Rector, by showing how sensitively his nature reacts to the thought of punitive pain. The syntax suggests that of an anxious small boy; instead of writing, 'It, and what Athy said too, made him cold and shivery to think of it', Joyce gives us the more concrete and frightening order of impressions: 'It made him shivery to think of it and cold: and what Athy said too.' The sensitivity of the language with its characteristically introverted anticipation of experience and its painful but courageous probing of sensations is all the more marked when we contrast it with the coarser, more extroverted reaction of the other boys which has immediately preceded the passage:

—No, no, said Athy. They'll both get it on the vital spot.
Wells rubbed himself and said in a crying voice:
—Please, sir, let me off!
Athy grinned and turned up the sleeves of his jacket, saying:

> It can't be helped;
> It must be done.
> So down with your breeches
> And out with your bum. (I, iv, pp. 45–6)

As so often in the novel, Stephen is set apart from others and his sensitive and imaginatively courageous, if anxious, questioning anticipates not only his bold visit to the Rector but the direction his youth and young adult life will take.

Against this subjective realism with which Stephen is presented in the opening chapter of *A Portrait of the Artist as a Young Man*, we must set the objective realism of the Christmas Party in the third section. The scene is set descriptively in this section and there are even occasional glimpses into Stephen's inner world as when he sits down after saying grace (I, iii, pp. 30–31), but the general method used in this section is a dramatic one; the main action and ideas are conveyed through dialogue. This method is appropriate since the section relates a row about religion and politics. The Christmas setting is seen to be ironic and the dialogue returns again and again to the same topics but, each time, a tone of increased bitterness raises the central conflict to a higher degree of dramatic power as the row mounts to a climax:

—Well, my Christmas dinner has been spoiled anyhow.

—There could be neither luck nor grace, Dante said, in a house where there is no respect for the pastors of the church.

Mr Dedalus threw his knife and fork noisily on his plate.

—Respect! he said. Is it for Billy with the lip or for the tub of guts up in Armagh? Respect!

—Princes of the church, said Mr Casey with slow scorn.

—Lord Leitrim's coachmen, yes, said Mr Dedalus.

—They are the Lord's anointed, Dante said. They are an honour to their country.

—Tub of guts, said Mr Dedalus coarsely. He has a handsome face, mind you, in repose. You should see that fellow lapping up his bacon and cabbage of a cold winter's day. O Johnny!

He twisted his features into a grimace of heavy bestiality and made a lapping noise with his lips.

—Really, Simon, said Mrs Dedalus, you should not speak that way before Stephen. It's not right.

—O, he'll remember all this when he grows up, said Dante hotly —the language he heard against God and religion and priests in his own home.

—Let him remember too, cried Mr Casey to her from across the table, the language with which the priests and the priests' pawns broke Parnell's heart and hounded him into his grave. Let him remember that too when he grows up.

—Sons of bitches! cried Mr Dedalus. When he was down they turned on him to betray him and rend him like rats in a sewer. Lowlived dogs! And they look it! By Christ, they look it!

—They behaved rightly, cried Dante. They obeyed their bishops and their priests. Honour to them!

—Well, it is perfectly dreadful to say that not even for one day in the year, said Mrs Dedalus, can we be free from these dreadful disputes! (I, iii, pp. 34–5)

Throughout this passage in which each character speaks directly for himself in his own words, in which Stephen is recalled only for an instant to be immediately forgotten again, and in which the squalid responses which the characters provoke in each other is presented with brutal frankness, the objectivity and realism are plain enough both in the sentiments and in the colloquial language in which they are expressed. Yet what is the purpose of this objective and realistic style at this point in the novel? Is it not precisely to set against the subjective realism of the other sections, to establish that Stephen's subjective world and the external objective world of family, nation, politics, and religion *really* do exist, for the confrontation, the irreconcilable collision of these two worlds is to provide the fundamental drama and meaning of the book?

The second chapter of the novel describes Stephen's adolescence from the earliest stirrings of sexuality to his first experience of intercourse with a prostitute and the chapter also recounts his growing alienation from his family, especially his father. The subjective and objective worlds begin to collide and appropriate styles convey the reality of each. During the banter between Heron and Stephen at Belvedere, the conclusion of the Whitsuntide play when Stephen turns away from his parents, and the visit to Cork when he feels his father's extroverted way of life challenge his own introversion, the pressure of an actual world is conveyed much of the time, as it is in the Christmas Party episode, through realistic dialogue. But there is also a brutal realism in a good deal of the description: 'The first sight of the filthy courtyard at Stradbrook with its foul green puddles and clots of liquid dung and steaming bran-troughs sickened Stephen's heart' (II, i, p. 65); 'A cry which was but the echo of an obscene scrawl which he had read on the oozing wall of a urinal' (II, v, p. 103); 'He had wandered into a maze of narrow and dirty streets. From the foul laneways he heard bursts of hoarse riot and wrangling and the drawling of drunken singers' (II, v, p. 103). Again, Joyce's symbolism can be as savagely and starkly cruel as the thing it represents as when Stephen goes home with the prostitute to have intercourse: 'Her room was warm and lightsome. A huge doll sat with her legs apart in the copious easychair beside the bed' (II, v, p. 103).

As for Stephen's subjective world, it is conveyed with the increased subtlety of insight into the more complex mind of the adolescent which we might have expected. The method sometimes verges on a formal kind of stream-of-consciousness or interior monologue:[1]

---

[1] Strictly speaking, stream-of-consciousness or interior monologue breaks away from formal grammar and syntax, yet it seems to me that the true heart of these techniques is the mental flux produced through the association of ideas rather than the absence of formal sentence structure. There is certainly a stage between pure analytical thinking in a character and stream-of-consciousness or interior monologue proper which has so far received no name, unless we use 'stream-of-consciousness' and 'interior monologue' as distinguishing terms, as M. H. Abrams, *A Glossary of Literary Terms* (New York, 1971), pp. 164–5, suggests. See also Leon Edel, *The Modern Psychological Novel* (New York, 1964); Melvin J. Friedman, *Stream of Consciousness: A Study in Literary Method* (New Haven, 1955); Robert Humphrey, *Stream of Consciousness in the Modern Novel* (Berkeley, 1954).

Stephen walked on at his father's side, listening to stories he had heard before, hearing again the names of the scattered and dead revellers who had been the companions of his father's youth. And a faint sickness sighed in his heart. He recalled his own equivocal position in Belvedere, a free boy, a leader afraid of his own authority, proud and sensitive and suspicious, battling against the squalor of his life and against the riot of his mind. The letters cut in the stained wood of the desk stared upon him, mocking his bodily weakness and futile enthusiasms and making him loathe himself for his own mad and filthy orgies. The spittle in his throat grew bitter and foul to swallow and the faint sickness climbed to his brain so that for a moment he closed his eyes and walked on in darkness.

He could still hear his father's voice. (II, iv, pp. 93–4)

And this manner of rendering Stephen's inner world is more flexible than it might seem. Thus, deliberate overwriting can convey the element of histrionic posturing in Stephen's over-reaction when he flees from his family after the play:

Without waiting for his father's questions he ran across the road and began to walk at breakneck speed down the hill. He hardly knew where he was walking. Pride and hope and desire like crushed herbs in his heart sent up vapours of maddening incense before the eyes of his mind. He strode down the hill amid the tumult of suddenrisen vapours of wounded pride and fallen hope and baffled desire. They streamed upwards before his anguished eyes in dense and maddening fumes and passed away above him till at last the air was clear and cold again. (II, iii, p. 89)

One of the most important themes of the second chapter is Stephen's adolescent romanticism, especially an idealization of sexuality and the shattering upsurge of a raw and brutal sexual appetite. Stephen's romanticism, epitomized by his regard for the poet Byron and his relationships with Mercedes and E.C. is aptly caught in the vague abstractions and breathless idealizations of language like the following:

He returned to Mercedes and, as he brooded upon her image, a strange unrest crept into his blood. Sometimes a fever gathered within him and led him to rove alone in the evening along the quiet avenue. The peace of the gardens and the kindly lights in the windows poured a tender influence into his restless heart. The noise of children at play annoyed him and their silly voices made him feel, even more keenly than he had felt at Clongowes, that he was different from others. He

did not want to play. He wanted to meet in the real world the un-
substantial image which his soul so constantly beheld. He did not know
where to seek it or how: but a premonition which led him on told
him that this image would, without any overt act of his, encounter
him. They would meet quietly as if they had known each other and
had made their tryst, perhaps at one of the gates or in some more
secret place. They would be alone, surrounded by darkness and
silence: and in that moment of supreme tenderness he would be
transfigured. He would fade into something impalpable under her
eyes and then in a moment, he would be transfigured. Weakness and
timidity and inexperience would fall from him in that magic moment.
(II, i, pp. 66-7)

In two ways, we must beware of considering this false. First, it accurately
conveys the fantasy quality of the boy's idealization of the sexual object
and the sexual relationship with its powerful sense of ethereal magic.
Secondly, such a daydream, even an intuition, of transfiguration—for all
the futility of its realization with a real mate in the external world—does
foreshadow (albeit in a weaker form) the more mature experience of the
anima-like image in the wading girl episode which is the grand transfiguration of Stephen's life in *A Portrait of the Artist as a Young Man*.
  What Thomas Hardy in his Preface to the first edition of *Jude the
Obscure* (1895) called the 'deadly war waged between flesh and spirit' is
carried into the closing pages of Joyce's second chapter of *A Portrait*, the
ethereal dream jarred and shocked by awakening starts of brutal passion:

A figure that had seemed to him by day demure and innocent came
towards him by night through the winding darkness of sleep, her face
transfigured by a lecherous cunning, her eyes bright with brutish joy.
Only the morning pained him with its dim memory of dark orgiastic
riot, its keen and humiliating sense of transgression. . . . Only at times,
in the pauses of his desire, when the luxury that was wasting him gave
room to a softer languor, the image of Mercedes traversed the back-
ground of his memory. . . . A tender premonition touched him of the
tryst he had then looked forward to and, in spite of the horrible reality
which lay between his hope of then and now, of the holy encounter
he had then imagined at which weakness and timidity and inexperience were to fall from him.
  Such moments passed and the wasting fires of lust sprang up again.
(II, v, pp. 101-2)

But in the third chapter of *A Portrait of the Artist as a Young Man*, which describes Stephen's growing consciousness of a state of mortal sin, the effect of Father Arnall's sermons on him, his repentance, confession, and absolution, the subjective world of pride and lust is confronted by the objective world again in the form of the institutions and teachings of the Church, transforming Stephen's inner world from cold indifference to one of terror and guilt, horror and remorse. Once again, the objective world is conveyed by a dramatic method, that of Father Arnall's sermons on death and judgement and the nature and torments of hell which are properly and powerfully presented in direct speech, and there is, of course, an ironic pointedness in these sermons which relates them dramatically to Stephen's sinful state. The sermons are masterpieces of oratory and exploit the rhetorical resources of language to the full. Thus, in conveying the physical torments of hell, Father Arnall objectifies these torments by recourse to a concreteness and immediacy particularly calculated (by Joyce) to impinge upon the senses of so acutely sensitive a youth as Stephen while the crushing hyperboles with which damnation is described are likely to weigh upon him in just proportion to the sheer enormity of his sense of guilt:

—The horror of this strait and dark prison is increased by its awful stench. All the filth of the world, all the offal and scum of the world, we are told, shall run there as to a vast reeking sewer when the terrible conflagration of the last day has purged the world. The brimstone too which burns there in such prodigious quantity fills all hell with its intolerable stench; and the bodies of the damned themselves exhale such a pestilential odour that as saint Bonaventure says, one of them alone would suffice to infect the whole world. The very air of this world, that pure element, becomes foul and unbreathable when it has been long enclosed. Consider then what must be the foulness of the air of hell. Imagine some foul and putrid corpse that has lain rotting and decomposing in the grave, a jellylike mass of liquid corruption. Imagine such a corpse a prey to flames, devoured by the fire of burning brimstone and giving off dense choking fumes of nauseous loathsome decomposition. And then imagine this sickening stench, multiplied a millionfold and a millionfold again from the millions upon millions of fetid carcasses massed together in the reeking darkness, a huge and rotting human fungus. Imagine all this and you will have some idea of the horror of the stench of hell. (III, ii, pp. 123–4)

Father Arnall uses analogy forcefully here but even more strikingly when he comes to describe the spiritual torments of hell, a rhetoric which

wrings the last pangs of mental agony out of the more subtle and intellectual side of Stephen's imagination:

> —Last and crowning torture of all the tortures of that awful place
> is the eternity of hell. Eternity! O, dread and dire word. Eternity!
> What mind of man can understand it? And remember, it is an
> eternity of pain. Even though the pains of hell were not so terrible as
> they are yet they would become infinite as they are destined to last for
> ever. But while they are everlasting they are at the same time, as you
> know, intolerably intense, unbearably extensive. To bear even the
> sting of an insect for all eternity would be a dreadful torment. What
> must it be, then, to bear the manifold tortures of hell for ever? For
> ever! For all eternity! Not for a year or for an age but for ever. Try to
> imagine the awful meaning of this. You have often seen the sand on
> the seashore. How fine are its tiny grains! And how many of those tiny
> little grains go to make up the small handful which a child grasps in
> its play. Now imagine a mountain of that sand, a million miles high,
> reaching from the earth to the farthest heavens, and a million miles
> broad, extending to remotest space, and a million miles in thickness:
> and imagine such an enormous mass of countless particles of sand
> multiplied as often as there are leaves in the forest, drops of water in the
> mighty ocean, feathers on birds, scales on fish, hairs on animals, atoms
> in the vast expanse of the air: and imagine that at the end of every
> million years a little bird came to that mountain and carried away in
> its beak a tiny grain of that sand. How many millions upon millions
> of centuries would pass before that bird had carried away even a square
> foot of that mountain, how many eons upon eons of ages before it had
> carried away all. Yet at the end of that immense stretch of time not
> even one instant of eternity could be said to have ended. At the end of
> all those billions and trillions of years eternity would have scarcely
> begun. And if that mountain rose again after it had been all carried away
> and if the bird came again and carried it all away again grain by grain:
> and if it so rose and sank as many times as there are stars in the sky,
> atoms in the air, drops of water in the sea, leaves on the trees, feathers
> upon birds, scales upon fish, hairs upon animals, at the end of all those
> innumerable risings and sinkings of that immeasurably vast mountain
> not one single instant of eternity could be said to have ended; even
> then, at the end of such a period, after that eon of time the mere thought
> of which makes our very brain reel dizzily, eternity would have scarcely
> begun. (III, ii, pp. 135-6)

The sheer oppressiveness of this vision is such that one scarcely notices
the rhetorical means by which it is reinforced, the constant alliteration

and assonance, the repetition, the parallel constructions, the ponderous rhythms.

Stephen's reactions, his inner world, is rendered by a method close to a stream-of-consciousness or interior monologue technique[2] which, if it is more formally literary than that used in *Ulysses*, is still flexible enough to catch every twist and turn of Stephen's long drawn out spiritual turmoil. It begins with the hardness of the uncontrite heart: 'A cold lucid indifference reigned in his soul. . . . What did it avail to pray when he knew that his soul lusted after its own destruction?' (III, i, pp. 106, 107). But every occasion has begun to inform against him and even a mathematical exercise at school reveals to him that the root of his trouble is not so much lust as a 'certain pride. . . . His pride in his own sin' (III, i, p. 107), which obstinately turns away from the possibility of forgiveness:

> The equation on the page of his scribbler began to spread out a widening tail, eyed and starred like a peacock's; and, when the eyes and stars of its indices had been eliminated, began slowly to fold itself together again. The indices appearing and disappearing were eyes opening and closing: the eyes opening and closing were stars being born and being quenched. The vast cycle of starry life bore his weary mind outward to its verge and inward to its centre, a distant music accompanying him outward and inward. What music? The music came nearer and he recalled the words, the words of Shelley's fragment upon the moon wandering companionless, pale for weariness. The stars began to crumble and a cloud of fine stardust fell through space.
>
> The dull light fell more faintly upon the page whereon another equation began to unfold itself slowly and to spread abroad its widening tail. It was his own soul going forth to experience, unfolding itself sin by sin, spreading abroad the balefire of its burning stars and folding back upon itself, fading slowly, quenching its own lights and fires. They were quenched: and the cold darkness filled chaos. (III, i, p. 106)

There is more here than metaphor and simile. Through the image of the peacock, pride is indicated with the concrete pictorialism of the old emblematic art. Yet the imagery is more complex and profound than might at first appear. Mathematics is the language of pure, unemotive, even cold, logic, while pride, and Stephen's pride in particular, is the most intellectual of the seven deadly sins. Furthermore, in the cosmic imagery which develops is suggested not only the growth but the magnitude of Stephen's obsessive megalomania and of his sin, for it is

[2] See above, footnote on p. 41.

the cardinal sin, the sin for which Lucifer, the brightest star in the firma-
ment of heaven, together with a third of the angels, fell—an echo of
which is perhaps conveyed in 'The stars began to crumble and a cloud of
fine stardust fell through space.'

The terrifying vision of damnation which follows Father Arnall's
sermons and prompts Stephen's contrition has been quoted earlier in this
study and there is space for only one more example which will show how
the method close to interior monologue[3] acutely records Stephen's
agony:

> Every word of it was for him. Against his sin, foul and secret, the
> whole wrath of God was aimed. The preacher's knife had probed
> deeply into his diseased conscience and he felt now that his soul was
> festering in sin. Yes, the preacher was right. God's turn had come. Like
> a beast in its lair his soul had lain down in its own filth but the blasts of
> the angel's trumpet had driven him forth from the darkness of sin into
> the light. The words of doom cried by the angel shattered in an instant
> his presumptuous peace. The wind of the last day blew through his
> mind; his sins, the jeweleyed harlots of his imagination, fled before the
> hurricane, squeaking like mice in their terror and huddled under a
> mane of hair.
>
> As he crossed the square, walking homeward, the light laughter of a
> girl reached his burning ear. The frail gay sound smote his heart more
> strongly than a trumpetblast, and, not daring to lift his eyes, he turned
> aside and gazed, as he walked, into the shadow of the tangled shrubs.
> Shame rose from his smitten heart and flooded his whole being. The
> image of Emma appeared before him and, under her eyes, the flood of
> shame rushed forth anew from his heart. If she knew to what his mind
> had subjected her or how his brutelike lust had torn and trampled
> upon her innocence! Was that boyish love? Was that chivalry? Was
> that poetry? The sordid details of his orgies stank under his very
> nostrils: the sootcoated packet of pictures which he had hidden in the
> flue of the fire-place and in the presence of whose shameless or bashful
> wantonness he lay for hours sinning in thought and deed; his monstrous
> dreams, peopled by apelike creatures and by harlots with gleaming
> jewel eyes; the foul long letters he had written in the joy of guilty
> confession and carried secretly for days and days only to throw them
> under cover of night among the grass in the corner of a field or beneath
> some hingeless door or in some niche in the hedges where a girl might
> come upon them as she walked by and read them secretly. Mad! Mad!
> Was it possible he had done these things? A cold sweat broke out

[3] See above, footnote on p. 41.

upon his forehead as the foul memories condensed within his brain.
(III, ii, pp. 118–19)

Although the style in this passage is in many respects still formal, pre-
serving the orthodox syntax and grammar of the literary sentence in
fiction, it also does contain some of the important features of the stream-
of-consciousness or interior monologue technique which Joyce uses later
in *Ulysses*. And we can see that the effect Joyce is after in the passage is
articulated through these features: the basic association of ideas, for
instance, under the pressure, here, of a powerful guilt—the angry word
of God in the preacher's mouth that suggests the angel's apocalyptic
trumpet, merging in turn into the girl's laughter which recalls scattered
memories of various secret sexual sins, one after the other, and distils
them into a single agonized consciousness of self-pollution.

The narrative method we have described as approaching stream-of-
consciousness and interior monologue[4] predominates throughout the
fourth chapter and this is highly appropriate to the subject matter. For
this chapter records the grand turning-point in Stephen's spiritual life,
and the action is either subjective or carries an entirely subjective
significance. If the theme of the preceding chapter is sin and damnation,
the theme of this chapter is salvation through vocation. Yet such a theme
is complex and linked to the former theme, since a sense of bogus
salvation through the false call to the priesthood gives way to a genuine
salvation through the authentic vocation of a wholly dedicated artist.

An impression of bogus salvation and a false call is rendered stylistically
through ironic modes of expression and highly artificial, overstrained,
and pompous language. An ironic gap is frequently implied between
Stephen's pious pretensions and the mundane, even squalid, realities of
daily life which constantly deflate them: 'The raw morning air whetted
his resolute piety; and often as he knelt among the few worshippers at the
side altar . . . he . . . imagined that he was kneeling at mass in the cata-
combs' (IV, i, p. 150). Tell-tale verbs which indicate appearance rather
than actuality point out the ironic truth about Stephen's spiritual state
and sense of religious vocation: 'Every part of his day, divided by what
he regarded now as the duties of his station in life, circled about its own
centre of spiritual energy. His life seemed to have drawn near to eternity'
(IV, i, p. 151). Ironic deflation may even sink to bathos, a bathos in which
heavenly aspiration is undermined by the most earthy of bodily func-
tions: 'To mortify his smell was more difficult as he found in himself no

---

[4] See above, footnote on p. 41.

instinctive repugnance to bad odours. . . . He found in the end that the only odour against which his sense of smell revolted was a certain stale fishy stink like that of longstanding urine: and whenever it was possible he subjected himself to this unpleasant odour' (IV, i, p. 154) 'His prayers and fasts availed him little for the suppression of anger at hearing his mother sneeze' (IV, i, p. 154). Pompous artificial language well illustrates the falseness of Stephen's attitude in the following: 'The rosaries too, which he said constantly—for he carried his beads loose in his trousers' pockets that he might tell them as he walked the streets—transformed themselves into coronals of flowers of such vague unearthly texture that they seemed to him as hueless and odourless as they were nameless' (IV, i, p. 151). But the most striking instance of false language indicating bogus attitude is Joyce's deliberate use of a high-flown laboured conceit with ludicrous echoes of the metaphysical style of the seventeenth century:

> . . . every thought, word and deed, every instance of consciousness could be made to revibrate radiantly in heaven: and at times his sense of such immediate repercussion was so lively that he seemed to feel his soul in devotion pressing like fingers the keyboard of a great cash register and to see the amount of his purchase start forth immediately in heaven, not as a number but as a frail column of incense or as a slender flower. (IV, i, p. 151)

By contrast, the power which authentic language lends the vision of genuine spiritual salvation later in this chapter has been so well illustrated in discussing the meaning of the novel in the early part of this study that it scarcely needs further comment. The third section of the fourth chapter, which culminates in the wading girl episode and the vision of the universe as a cosmic flower, blazes almost from beginning to end with the steady glory of authentic rhapsodic language. But we might note briefly in passing one or two devices of language by means of which Joyce helps to create and sustain his rhapsody. The repetition of the word of affirmation which begins the following passage, for instance, and the long list of qualifying epithets after the noun, 'thing', which steadily mount at the end of the passage to a climax of soaring ecstasy provide a good example: 'Yes! Yes! Yes! He would create proudly out of the freedom and power of his soul, as the great artificer whose name he bore, a living thing, new and soaring and beautiful, impalpable, imperishable' (IV, iii, p. 174). Again, the well-balanced repetition and inversion of the following is no mere precious affectation but helps to sustain the vision of Stephen as

Daedalus hovering rapturously on the wing: 'An ecstasy of flight made radiant his eyes and wild his breath and tremulous and wild and radiant his windswept limbs' (IV, iii, p. 173). Finally, in the paragraph which concludes the section and chapter on a quieter note, we might particularly observe the languorous cadences and the languidly drawn-out sentence at the end:

> He climbed to the crest of the sandhill and gazed about him. Evening had fallen. A rim of the young moon cleft the pale waste of sky like the rim of a silver hoop embedded in grey sand; and the tide was flowing in fast to the land with a low whisper of her waves, islanding a few last figures in distant pools. (IV, iii, p. 177)

The fifth chapter opens with what might seem an anticlimax after the rhapsody with which the fourth chapter concludes. Yet, as we shall see, the effect of anticlimax is intentional and the squalid domestic realism of the breakfast scenes at Stephen's home provides the deliberate antithesis of the last section of the previous chapter and of the passage which concludes the fifth chapter and the novel. The squalid realism is managed by appropriate language:

> The box of pawn tickets at his elbow had just been rifled and he took up idly one after another in his greasy fingers the blue and white dockets, scrawled and sanded and creased and bearing the name of the pledger as Daly or MacEvoy.
>
> 1 Pair Buskins.
> 1 D. Coat.
> 3 Articles and White.
> 1 Man's Pants.
>
> Then he put them aside and gazed throughoutfully at the lid of the box, speckled with louse marks....
>
> When the enamelled basin had been fitted into the well of the sink and the old washingglove flung on the side of it he allowed his mother to scrub his neck and root into the folds of his ears and into the interstices at the wings of his nose.
>
> —Well, it's a poor case, she said, when a university student is so dirty that his mother has to wash him. (V, i, pp. 177–8)

In this passage, the large proportion of simple and common monosyllabic words, one hundred and twelve as compared with thirty-three polysyllabic words, helps to stress the mundane quality of the scene and action. The scenes at the university, which follow, and those later in the third section at the library are presented by means of the objectively realistic style with which we are already familiar. There is considerable use of dramatic dialogue, both colloquial and formal, the colloquial dialogue capturing the ribald wit of the students, the more formal kinds of language expressing, aptly enough, the conversation of the Dean of Studies, the snatches of a lecture by the Professor of Science, and the intellectual discussion between Stephen and the other students, particularly the exposition of Stephen's ideas. Joyce's linguistic facility here displays a considerable range. Wittily, he exploits the saucy ambiguity of language:

—Let us take woman, said Stephen.
—Let us take her! said Lynch fervently. (V, i, p. 212)

Humorously, he deflates Temple's political enthusiasm for his hero, John Anthony Collins, with quick recourse to a child's vulgar street rhyme and a colloquial image drawn from horse-racing:

—And what about John Anthony's poor little sister:

> *Lottie Collins lost her drawers;*
> *Won't you kindly lend her yours?*

Stephen laughed and Moynihan, pleased with the result, murmured again:
—We'll have five bob each way on John Anthony Collins. (V, i, p. 201)

Furthermore, Joyce demonstrates a quick flexibility in switching from one kind of language to another, from the almost self-parody of the lecturer's speech, for example, with its heavy laboured attempt at a relieving joke, to the colloquial sexual innuendo caught up by the student, Moynihan, from the reference to 'balls', and thence to the more ponderous humour which Stephen's literary imagination begins to fashion in the form of an elaborate image:

—So we must distinguish between elliptical and ellipsoidal. Perhaps some of you gentlemen may be familiar with the works of Mr W. S. Gilbert. In one of his songs he speaks of the billiard sharp who is condemned to play:

On a cloth untrue
With a twisted cue
And elliptical billiard balls.

—He means a ball having the form of the ellipsoid of the principal axes of which I spoke a moment ago.

Moynihan leaned down towards Stephen's ear and murmured:

—What price ellipsoidal balls! Chase me, ladies, I'm in the cavalry!

His fellowstudent's rude humour ran like a gust through the cloister of Stephen's mind, shaking into gay life limp priestly vestments that hung upon the walls, setting them to sway and caper in a sabbath of misrule. (V, i, p. 196)

And the image, as it is developed subsequently, also echoes the laborious false humour of the professorial staff, though taken to the point of extravaganza: 'Kilting their gowns for leap frog, holding one another back, shaken with deep false laughter, smacking one another behind and laughing at their rude malice' (V, i, pp. 196–7).

The world of objective realism is no longer simply the world which confronts and oppresses Stephen's subjective vision, it is the world he must defeat if his individual being is to triumph. Exile does not mean merely running away, it means descending into the hell of Dublin first if he is to harrow his own soul. Poetry, as we see in the second section of the fifth chapter, is partly made from the external objective world. So, from the rapture of his vision in the fourth chapter, Stephen must descend into a confrontation with the squalor of his home life, into the society of his professors with their pedantic expertise and that of his fellow students with their trivial ribaldry and endless chatter about the nation, politics, religion, and sex, while he must also brave the tempting ghost of E.C., flitting through it all, haunting him with seductive promise. We may see in this chapter not only how the many themes of the book are marvellously woven into a unity but also how the organization of the material underscores the indivisible meaning of a single authentic fate. It is in collision with the external world that Stephen hammers out his theories about art, an intellectual position which must precede his composition of the villanelle[5] and his journey into exile:

[5] We should hardly be surprised if Stephen expresses himself in the artificial style and limited poetic sentiment of his time, with the elaborate and rather precious aestheticism of a Wilde or Dowson and in one of the intricate stanza forms imported from France during the eighteen-eighties and nineties, the particularly difficult form practised by W. E. Henley and Austin Dobson. Stephen is occupied on what all other ages but our own would expect an apprentice artist to be engaged on, learning his craft,

The feelings excited by improper art are kinetic, desire or loathing. Desire urges us to possess, to go to something; loathing urges us to abandon, to go from something. These are kinetic emotions. The arts which excite them, pornographical or didactic, are therefore improper arts. The esthetic emotion (I use the general term) is therefore static. The mind is arrested and raised above desire and loathing. (V, i, p. 209)

This is not simply an aesthetic theory. Behind it is a whole intellectual and, indeed, temperamental attitude, for we now see that Stephen's earlier alienation as a boy and his rather anti-social behaviour now among his fellow students is not without point. Just as art must avoid didacticism, pornography, and emotional contagion, so the artist must set himself apart from the equivalents of these dangers in the external world, from being overpowered by the claims of nation, politics, religion, family and, above all, by the kind of sexual experience that will inevitably lead to his being entrammelled by these other 'nets'. This is the ultimate meaning of Stephen's rejection of E.C. in the last three sections of his fifth chapter. She would keep his soul at home in a sterile Ireland. There is, for example, her flirtation with the priest, the sinister antithesis of all Stephen stands for: 'He had done well to leave her to flirt with her priest, to toy with a church which was the scullerymaid of christendom. . . . To him she would unveil her soul's shy nakedness, to one who was but schooled in the discharging of a formal rite rather than to him, a priest of eternal imagination, transmuting the daily bread of experience into the radiant body of everliving life' (V, ii, pp. 224, 225). The skilful dignified use of lofty phrases with sacramental associations is noteworthy here and, indeed, throughout the second section of this chapter Joyce returns appropriately to a rhapsodic grand style which conveys the ecstasy in which phallus becomes logos and erotic feeling and imagery is transmuted into the Word of art:

mastering technique, and it is natural that he should turn his early attention to poetry. Were we to judge Joyce, himself, by the body of his poetry, especially his early poetry (see, for example, Richard Ellmann, *James Joyce*, pp. 83–6), we should not rate him very highly. It is scarcely astonishing that the reach of Stephen's aesthetic, of his aspiration and his vision, should exceed the grasp of his verse; it would have been incredible and wholly unconvincing if Joyce had put into Stephen's mouth something of the calibre of Yeats's later poems, or Eliot's *The Wasteland*, or even Pound's *Sestina: Altaforte*, and it is inevitable, indeed, a commendable stroke of art, that the immature Stephen should, in his verse, fall far short of the accomplishment with which the mature Joyce, in poetic prose, expresses Stephen's vision.

The instant flashed forth like a point of light and now from cloud on cloud of vague circumstance confused form was veiling softly its afterglow. O! In the virgin womb of the imagination the word was made flesh. . . .

A glow of desire kindled again his soul and fired and fulfilled all his body. Conscious of his desire she was waking from odorous sleep, the temptress of his villanelle. Her eyes, dark and with a look of languor, were opening to his eyes. Her nakedness yielded to him, radiant, warm, odorous and lavish-limbed, enfolded him like a shining cloud, enfolded him like water with a liquid life: and like a cloud of vapour or like waters circumfluent in space the liquid letters of speech, symbols of the element of mystery, flowed forth over his brain. (V, ii, pp. 221, 227)

The sense here is underscored by onomatopoeic devices, by the foaming effect of the repeated letter 'f' at the beginning and end of the passage and the luxury of the soft rhetoric with its liquid sounds, particularly the profusion of the letters 'l' and 'w'.

The style of the diary fragments, with which the novel concludes, now and then comes closest yet to the stream-of-consciousness and interior monologue techniques of *Ulysses*: '5 *April*: Wild spring. Scudding clouds. O life! Dark stream of swirling bogwater on which appletrees have cast down their delicate flowers. Eyes of girls among the leaves. Girls demure and romping. All fair or auburn: no dark ones. They blush better. Houp-la!' (V, iv, p. 255). Yet there is no regressive decline into subjectivism in this. On the contrary, it represents, as does the villanelle, the artist's attempt to grapple with subjective reactions by setting them down, the beginning of the creation of an 'objective' world from inner experience: 'The personality of the artist, at first a cry or a cadence or a mood and then a fluid and lambent narrative, finally refines itself out of existence, impersonalizes itself, so to speak. The esthetic image in the dramatic form is life purified in and reprojected from the human imagination' (V, i, p. 219). This intellectual theory becomes a process of Stephen's inner life in his dream: 'Strange figures advance from a cave. They are not as tall as men. One does not seem to stand quite apart from another. Their faces are phosphorescent, with darker streaks. They peer at me and their eyes seem to ask me something. They do not speak' (V, iv, p. 254). Any interpretation of this dream fragment must remain tentative, yet the cave does suggest the creative matrix. The strange figures not so tall as men may represent the more primitive and alien or repressed forces within Stephen emerging from the collective unconscious or impersonal imagination and questioning the conscious ego of

Stephen with its purely personal standpoint. As yet these figures do not achieve verbal expression but the blend of luminosity and darkness in their faces perhaps hints at a union of opposites, an integration which will take place in Stephen's creative life whereby the personal and impersonal will find harmonious expression in an artistic *persona* to present to the world. The earlier dream fragment of 'the images of fabulous kings' certainly suggests the mythical or archetypal imagination, itself a highly impersonal form of expression, at work.

Critics have sometimes argued that, at best, Stephen's victory is meant ironically and, at worst, the overall mood of the novel is one of black despair. This is largely a looking towards the Stephen Dedalus of *Ulysses* and it would be equally as weak an argument to point to Joyce's own life, for nowhere do we find a writer with a greater conviction of his own artistic achievement.[6] Yet, if we cannot argue from Joyce's life we can note in *A Portrait of the Artist as a Young Man*, and indeed in its closing lines, an heroic temper which is there besides the comedy, the realism, and objectivity and which also characterized Joyce, the man and artist. It is no accident that *A Portrait of the Artist as a Young Man* and *Ulysses* are built up on the rock-like foundation of heroic legend. Stephen's character does not change radically in the course of the novel, it *develops*, and it develops from a firm basis of temperament—reserve becoming independence, pride growing into the self-assertion of individuality, sensitivity into the artistic personality, and so on.[7] Earlier in the novel, we have noted Stephen's courage as when, for example, he is able, despite his nervous sensitivity, to face the Rector. Romantic heroism is, of course, a feature of his adolescent daydreams: 'He sat listening to the words and following the ways of adventure that lay open in the coals, arches and vaults and winding galleries and jagged caverns' (II, ii, p. 70). But this romantic heroism is, quite early in Stephen's life, the motivating force behind his yearning for other places and the true beginning of his path to exile: 'The vastness and strangeness of the life

---

[6] If we were to go outside the novel, however, we might just as easily contend that the Stephen Dedalus of *A Portrait* became the great and successful artist, James Joyce rather than Stephen, the comparative failure, of *Ulysses*.

[7] A development which Joyce particularly intended, as Richard Ellmann, *James Joyce*, p. 306, points out, 'The book's pattern, as he explained to Stanislaus, is that we are what we were; our maturity is an extension of our childhood', and, as Ellmann, p. 307, adds, this is development: '*A Portrait of the Artist as a Young Man* is in fact the gestation of a soul, and in the metaphor Joyce found his new principle of order.'

suggested to him by the bales of merchandise stocked along the walls or swung aloft out of the holds of steamers wakened again in him the unrest which had sent him wandering in the evening from garden to garden in search of Mercedes' (II, ii, p. 68). The desire for woman here does not lead to E.C. but to the wading girl, to the union of Stephen with his own soul-image. A romantic heroism is implied in Joyce's most succinct expression of the novel's subject, 'the adventure in his mind' (II, iii, p. 79), for the man who faces the inner adventure of himself is truly romantic, truly heroic.[8]

Certainly, in his very earliest draft of the novel, the manuscript auto-biographical essay, entitled 'A Portrait of the Artist' (MS. at Buffalo, collated with Stanislaus Joyce's typed copy of the imperfect MS. at Cornell, and cited in *The Workshop of Daedalus*, pp. 60–74), later developed into *Stephen Hero*, Joyce relates how his artist deliberately affirmed a positive and idealistic vision in particular despite of his mastery of art in irony and an asceticism of intellect. This vision appears to anticipate much of the development of Stephen's image of woman in the final version of *A Portrait*, including the motifs of poetic tribute to a beloved, the comedy of meetings with her, her appearance in the artist's dreams, boyhood preoccupation with sexuality, a communication through, yet transcending, lust, and the emergence of a transcendental image of woman which helps commitment to life (in a phrase, 'an envoy from the fair courts of life' which links the image with the wading girl of the final version), offers tenderness and love, refines passion, enriches the soul, and is saluted as a semi-divine being, a secular kind of Virgin Mary, who in her sacramental aspect provides grace and salvation and a union characterized by rapture, by a heavenly experience of soaring flight. It may also be significant that this episode in the manuscript of 'A Portrait' immediately follows a version of the incident on the strand and its effect on the development of Stephen's aesthetic sensibility. Obviously, the final version of the novel must ultimately be interpreted in its own terms and not by the intention of an earlier version, yet the similar design and

---

[8] We need not be unduly perturbed by Stephen's wish to escape from what he describes as romantic art in the fragment of *Stephen Hero*, since what remains here is so alien, in many ways, to the mood and spiritual pattern of *A Portrait* and was rejected as unsatisfactory, whereas, in the final version of the novel, Joyce returns to something like the mood and pattern of the earliest version, the essay story, 'A Portrait of the Artist'. All of which is not to deny that the final version shows a fine wholesome balance of what we might call 'romantic' and 'classical' elements if these were not so notoriously imprecise terms.

mood and, above all, the plain statement in the earlier version of the paramountcy of the positive and idealistic vision in the face of ironic art and ascetic intellect is striking and it is all the more striking when we consider the absence of a rhetoric of irony in the later crucial passages of idealistic affirmation in the final version, a rhetoric which some critics appear to be importing arbitrarily from other parts of the novel:

> Dearest of mortals! In spite of tributary verses and of the comedy of meetings here and in the foolish society of sleep the fountain of being (it seemed) had been interfused. Years before, in boyhood, the energy of sin opening a world before him, he had been made aware of thee . . . in all that ardent adventure of lust didst thou not even then communicate? Beneficent one! (the shrewdness of love was in the title) thou camest timely, as a witch to the agony of the self-devourer, an envoy from the fair courts of life. How could he thank thee for that enrichment of soul by thee consummated? Mastery of art had been achieved in irony; asceticism of intellect had been a mood of indignant pride: but who had revealed him to himself but thou alone? In ways of tenderness, simple, intuitive tenderness, thy love had made to arise in him the central torments of life. Thou hadst put thine arms about him and, intimately prisoned as thou hadst been, in the soft stir of thy bosom, the raptures of silence, the murmured words, thy heart had spoken to his heart. Thy disposition could refine and direct his passion, holding mere beauty at the cunningest angle. Thou wert sacramental, imprinting thine indelible mark, of very visible grace. A litany must honour thee; Lady of the Apple Trees, Kind Wisdom, Sweet Flower of Dusk. . . . The blood hurries to a gallop in his veins; his nerves accumulate an electric force; he is footed with flame. A kiss: and they leap together, indivisible, upwards, radiant lips and eyes, their bodies sounding with the triumph of harps! Again, beloved! Again, thou bride! Again, ere life is ours! (MS. of 'A Portrait of the Artist' at Buffalo, pp. 10–11; cited in *Workshop of Daedalus*, pp. 65–6)

Again, in the romantic and heroic affirmation of life with which *Ulysses* ends, the only irony lies in the confrontation between the conclusion of this novel and all the squalor that precedes it, for the novel does not end with squalor but with beauty and courage in the face of life and love. Similarly, if we are to read the text of *A Portrait of the Artist as a Young Man* faithfully, if we are to listen to its language and its rhetoric, if we are to weigh its ultimate comment and consider its final place in the novel's scheme, contrasting it with the squalor with which the fifth chapter begins, how can we read the final passage otherwise than as an affirmation of romantic heroism without a trace of irony directed against Stephen? And this positive reading of the final entries in Stephen's diary is strengthened when we observe that they follow immediately upon the final meeting with and rejection of E.C.:

16 April: Away! Away!

The spell of arms and voices: the white arms of roads, their promise of close embraces and the black arms of tall ships that stand against the moon, their tale of distant nations. They are held out to say: We are alone. Come. And the voices say with them: We are your kinsmen. And the air is thick with their company as they call to me, their kinsman, making ready to go, shaking the wings of their exultant and terrible youth.[9]

26 April: Mother is putting my new secondhand clothes in order. She prays now, she says, that I may learn in may own life and away from home and friends what the heart is and what it feels. Amen. So be it. Welcome, O life! I go to encounter for the millionth time the reality of experience and to forge in the smithy of my soul the uncreated conscience of my race.

27 April: Old father, old artificer, stand me now and ever in good stead. (V, iv, p. 257)

Let such language speak for itself. It is only the cultural nihilists of our time who could confuse literature with mere cleverness, or believe that a constant and destructive disbelief is the essence of the creative act, or fail to see that great and enduring art is an act of heroic faith. A sceptical irony, today's obssession, is but one eye in the artist's stereoscopic gaze and Joyce, no more than any true novelist, wishes to dissolve his world into nothing. Such a superior despair, infinitely colder than Stephen's young and understandable lack of compassion, only succeeds in mocking itself and it leaves intact the idealism and aspiration of youth which curiously remains to season the veteran stuff of our real maturity. Critics may prefer a world of depreciation, cynicism, and cowardice, and

[9] The erotic imagery in this passage reveals that characteristic displacement of energy from a sexual objective to a cultural task which Freud called sublimation and Jung described as the transition, through the 'reconciling symbol' or 'transcendant function', from the erotic attachment to woman to the service of the soul; see the analysis of the *Shepherd* of Hermas, a classic case which throws considerable light on Stephen's spiritual development, in C. G. Jung, *Psychological Types*, tr. H. Godwin Baynes (London, 1946), pp. 275–97, 608–10, rev. R. F. C. Hull (1971), pp. 224–40, 479–81.

we cannot answer for whatever their minds reflect back at them, but the truly imaginative soul confronting the destiny of its own Self is another matter, as Joyce shows us he knew only too well, an adventure in the mind in which depreciation, cynicism, and cowardice in all their squalor have been outfaced and surpassed.

Select Bibliography

A EDITIONS

A Portrait of the Artist as a Young Man (first publ. New York: Ben Huebsch, 1916; London: Jonathan Cape, 1924; Harmondsworth: Penguin, 1960). The Definitive Text (used throughout the present study), corrected from the Dublin Holograph by Chester G. Anderson and ed. Richard Ellmann (London: Jonathan Cape, 1968).

Stephen Hero, Theodore Spencer (ed.) (Norfolk, Connecticut: New Directions, 1944). A New Edition Incorporating the Additional Manuscript Pages in the Yale University Library, ed. John J. Slocum and Herbert Cahoon (Norfolk, Connecticut: New Directions, 1955 and London: Cape, 1956); a few more additional pages incorporated (New Directions, 1959).

Epithanies, Oscar A. Silverman (ed.) (Buffalo: Lockwood Memorial Library, 1956).

B BIOGRAPHY AND LETTERS

ELLMANN, RICHARD, *James Joyce* (New York: Oxford University Press, 1959).

GILBERT, STUART and ELLMANN, RICHARD (eds.), *Letters of James Joyce*, 3 vols. (London: Faber, 1957–66). S. Gilbert (ed.), vol. I (1957). R. Ellmann (ed.), vols. II and III (1966).

C BIBLIOGRAPHY

SLOCUM, JOHN and CAHOON, HERBERT, *A Bibliography of Joyce, 1882–1941* (New Haven, Connecticut: Yale University Press and London: Hart-Davis, 1953).

BEEBE, MAURICE and LITZ, WALTON, 'Criticism of James Joyce', *Modern Fiction Studies*, IV (Spring, 1958), 71–99; and, with PHILLIP F. HERRING, 'Criticism of Joyce: A Selected Checklist', *MFS*, XV (Spring, 1969), 105–82.

DEMING, ROBERT H., *A Bibliography of James Joyce Studies* (Lawrence: University of Kansas Libraries, 1964).

STALEY, THOMAS P. (ed.), *The James Joyce Quarterly* (Tulsa, Oklahoma: University of Tulsa, 1963–).

D STUDIES AND CRITICISM

ANDERSON, C. G., 'The Sacrificial Butter', *Accent*, XII (Winter, 1952), 3–13.

——, *A Word-Index to James Joyce's Stephen Hero* (Ridgefield, Connecticut: Ridgebury Press, 1958).

BEEBE, MAURICE, 'Joyce and Aquinas: The Theory of Aesthetics', *Philological Quarterly*, XXXVI (January, 1957), 20–35.

BLOCK, HASKELL M., 'The Critical Theory of James Joyce', *Journal of Aesthetics and Art Criticism*, VIII (March, 1950), 172–84.

BOYD, ELIZABETH F., 'Joyce's Hell-Fire Sermons', *Modern Language Notes*, LXXV (November, 1960), 561–71.

CONNOLLY, THOMAS E. (ed.), *Joyce's 'Portrait': Criticisms and Critiques* (New York: Appleton-Century-Crofts, 1962).

DAICHES, DAVID, *The Novel and the Modern World*, revised edn. (University of Chicago Press: Chicago and Cambridge University Press: Cambridge, 1960), pp. 83–90.

DEMING, ROBERT H. (ed.), *James Joyce: The Critical Heritage*, 2 vols. (London: Routledge and Kegan Paul, 1970).

EPSTEIN, EDMUND L., *The Ordeal of Stephen Dedalus* (Carbondale: South Illinois University Press, 1971).

GIVENS, SEON (ed.), *James Joyce: Two Decades of Criticism* (New York: Vanguard Press, 1948).

GOLDBERG, S. L., *Joyce* (Edinburgh: Oliver and Boyd, 1962), pp. 47–63.

HENDRY [CHAYES], IRENE, 'Joyce's Epiphanies', *Sewanee Review*, LIV (Summer, 1946), 1–19.

JACK, JANE H., 'Art and the *Portrait of the Artist*', *Essays in Criticism*, V (October, 1955), 354–64.

KAIN, RICHARD M. and SCHOLES, ROBERT E. (eds.), *The Workshop of Daedalus: James Joyce and the Raw Materials for A Portrait of the Artist as a Young Man* (Evanston: Northwestern University Press, 1965).

MAGALANER, MARVIN (ed.), *A James Joyce Miscellany* (New York: The James Joyce Society, 1957), 3rd series (Carbondale: Southern Illinois University Press, 1962).

——, and KAIN, RICHARD M., *Joyce: The Man, the Work, the Reputation* (New York: New York University Press, 1956), pp. 102–29.

MORRIS, WILLIAM E. and NAULT, CLIFFORD A. (eds.), *Portraits of an Artist* (New York: The Odyssey Press, 1962).

NOON, WILLIAM, *Joyce and Aquinas* (New Haven: Yale University Press, 1957), pp. 18–59.

PRESCOTT, JOSEPH, 'James Joyce: A Study in Words', *PMLA*, LIV (March, 1939), 304–15.

——, 'James Joyce's Stephen Hero', *Journal of English and Germanic Philology*, LIII (April, 1954), 214–23.

REDFORD, GRANT H., 'The Role of Structure in Joyce's "Portrait"', *Modern Fiction Studies*, IV (Spring, 1958), 21–30.

SEWARD, BARBARA, 'The Artist and the Rose', *University of Toronto Quarterly*, XXVI (January, 1957), 180–90.

STEWART, J. I. M., *Eight Modern Writers* (Oxford: Clarendon Press, 1963), pp. 438–50.

TINDALL, WILLIAM YORK, *A Reader's Guide to James Joyce* (New York: Noonday Press and London: Thames and Hudson, 1959), pp. 50–103.

VAN GHENT, DOROTHY, *The English Novel: Form and Content* (New York: Holt, Rinehart and Winston, 1953), pp. 263–76, 463–73.

Index